Profiles in Character

Twenty-six Stories That Will Instruct and Inspire Teenagers

Edited by
Max Malikow

UNIVERSITY PRESS OF AMERICA,® INC.
Lanham • Boulder • New York • Toronto • Plymouth, UK

Copyright © 2008 by
University Press of America,® Inc.
4501 Forbes Boulevard
Suite 200
Lanham, Maryland 20706
UPA Acquisitions Department (301) 459-3366

Estover Road
Plymouth PL6 7PY
United Kingdom

Library of Congress Control Number: 2007927904
ISBN-13: 978-0-7618-3686-5 (clothbound : alk. paper)
ISBN-10: 0-7618-3686-1 (clothbound : alk. paper)
ISBN-13: 978-0-7618-3687-2 (paperback : alk. paper)
ISBN-10: 0-7618-3687-X (paperback : alk. paper)

To SC: You have all of the admirable qualities addressed in this book–
and more.

To Dr. Ronald H. Wright: Your excellent advice made this book
possible. You told me to look to the future, rather than obsess over the
past. Your wisdom and compassion have made a difference in my life.

TABLE OF CONTENTS

    Blindsided (Richard Cohen)
    Journalist Richard Cohen is a blind cancer survivor with
    multiple sclerosis. Living in a culture that favors health,
    beauty, and independence, he describes his redefinition
    of what it means to be a man.

Tragic Optimism
In a Nazi concentration camp Holocaust survivor and
psychiatrist Viktor Frankl formulated a philosophy of
life that sustained him and instructs us on how to cope
with pain, guilt, and death.

Abraham Lincoln's Depression
The President managed to meet his awesome
responsibilities in spite of a profound, unremitting
clinical depression.

Foreword

Teaching morals, values and ideals for developing a student's character has a long tradition in American schools. Increasingly, however, how educators approach the teaching of values and morals has become contested ground. In my own nearly half century as a student and teacher in public and private schools, I have experienced approaches ranging from pure indoctrination of absolute beliefs to a much less direct, but equally intentional, strategy to clarify a student's personal values.

Educational programs rise and fall in popularity with cultural and political climates, but an unavoidable realization is that all education is character education. What we teach, how we choose to teach it, and how we become to behave with each other, and with students, finds the teacher at center stage. Max Malikow's experiences as a teacher and a teacher educator are a testament to this. In the tradition of great teachers, he recognizes the power of stories for promoting thoughtful discussions, discussions involving the complexities and contradictions of real people deciding on real circumstances. Books like Max's are always needed, but especially so now.

In a society which for some may seem adrift, Max's selection and arrangement of stories can help students learn how to navigate the waters between the seemingly solid shores of fixed and rigid truths and the murkier and more variated cultural geography of contingencies. The questions he poses from each story invite students and teachers to engage in thoughtful conversations, the core activity of thoughtful teaching. Students need to talk and be heard. By sharing, and by learning how others come to have a certain perspective, these discussions can change how one thinks, and, often, what one thinks.

Max is a teacher, and a teacher deeply concerned for others. This book represents his concern. He does not impose ready-made answers, but neither does his selection of stories and questions leave one with the idea that there are no values upon which we can commonly agree. It has all the important elements a teacher needs for guiding students in their human quest.

Stephen Fleury, Ph.D.
Professor of Education
Le Moyne College

Preface

Whenever I hear writers explain why they write, I pay close attention. Some describe writing as part of an effort to make sense of something – a kind of thinking out loud. Others characterize it as a means of self-expression; just as artists and musicians express themselves in their creative works. Many speak of writing as a compulsion – something they simply have to do. This book, written in the wake of a great personal disappointment, issued forth from the compulsion to make sense of something.

The writing of this book proved to be therapeutic. It moved me to reflect on the kind of man I want to be and qualities that man would have. I found healing in considering the stories of people who have demonstrated the qualities of adaptability, courage, endurance, integrity, perseverance, responsibility, and wisdom. It is my hope that these stories contribute to the personal growth of all who read them.

Max Malikow
Syracuse, New York
August, 2006

Acknowledgements

Help and encouragement in this writing project came from people – "rainy day people" as singer-songwriter Gordon Lightfoot characterized such helpers. Some of my "rainy day people" are colleagues: Robert Anderson, William Day, Maria DiTullio, Antonio Eppolito, Eric Holzwarth, Steve Fleury, Norb Henry, Michael Kagan, and Wen Ma. Other "rainy day people" are special friends: Tracy Brown, Mary Capocefalo, Rabbi Earl Grollman, and Father Robert Scully.

My brother Marvin and sister-in-law Evelyn have always been supportive of and interested in my work. Last, and certainly not least, is my Rachel Joy, who typed this manuscript on her summer vacation from Eastern University.

Permissions

Introduction

This is a book written by a teacher for teachers. It is not a stretch to say that I have been writing this book for thirty-four years. Over the years I have accumulated countless stories that serve as illustrations of the traits that contribute to admirable character. This volume is a compilation of the twenty-six most effective of these stories. By effective, I mean classroom-tested stories that have generated enthusiastic classroom discussion through the years. These stories have moved and inspired hundreds of my students. In contemporary pedagogical terminology, these stories have proven effective for *teaching in the affective domain*.

When character education is discussed, the inevitable question is: "Whose values will be taught?" The values presented in this book are everybody's values. There are many values that have been affirmed as virtuous by all people, religious and nonreligious alike, regardless of when and where they have lived. Concerning religious based values, as one who has taught comparative religions, I am confident in stating that the world's religions are virtually identical in their ethical teaching in spite of their considerable theological diversity.

I agree with Aristotle's characterization of a virtue as the apex between two vices. This Aristotelian sentiment is expressed by the adage: "Great strengths are great weaknesses and the reverse is true as well." This book consists of one to three stories for each of seventeen character traits. The stories average three pages in length and all of them can be read in less than five minutes. (The discussions can go on forever!)

There are discussion questions following each of the stories along with suggested follow-up activities recommending assignments, guest speakers, other stories, books, movies, and movie excerpts.

Profiles in Character is intended for high school students as part of their character education. Each story and its discussion questions are designed as a twenty-minute lesson. (The suggested follow-up activities are not included in this time estimate.) Given the one-hundred-and-eighty days of a school year, this book provides enough material to make a substantial contribution to a character education curriculum.

Although intended for educational use, these stories have the potential to inspire anyone. It is my hope that this book reaches a wider audience and finds a place in a bookstore's *inspiration* or *self-help* section.

Chapter I

Adaptability

BLINDSIDED (RICHARD COHEN)

Was nich nicht umbringt, macht mich starker.
(That which does not kill me, makes me stronger.)
                                    - Friedrich Wilhelm Nietzsche

Richard Cohen knows professional success, having risen to the top of his profession in both print and television journalism. Also, he is familiar with good health, which is now a memory. In adulthood he has survived two bouts with cancer, lost his eyesight, and is now experiencing life in a body continually deteriorating from multiple sclerosis. In spite of all that he has lost, he has retained the determination to be a good father and husband and enjoy the pleasures of life that are available to him. To succeed at this determination he has had to redefine for himself what it means to be a man. In a single word, he has had to be adaptable. The following is an excerpt from the memoir, Blindsided.

I feel weak because I acknowledge the realities of my life. We exist in a culture that celebrates strength. Men are strong and self-reliant. I am weakened and need the help of others. There is no escape from the rust I see on my body.

I must rise above the culture of perfection and remember that I can be even if I can no longer *do*. I am learning to acknowledge weakness,

1

accept assistance, and discover new forms of self-definition. My formula has changed. I do not read self-absorbed men's magazines or go to Vin Diesel movies. A new male ideal will have to do and might even save me. I cannot allow myself to be held captive by old dreams.

Success comes today by a different standard, measured by more cerebral achievements and often centered on the lives of my children. Those kids *are* the center of my life. Careers evolve into jobs, and sooner or later it becomes apparent to most of us that there is a lot more to life than professional recognition. Dealing with challenges to health is a great ally in nurturing that change in priorities.

Seeing the suffering that comes from illness—and it is all around me—has changed me. It has softened me, though Meredith might not believe that. What I want my children to learn has come into sharp relief. I want them to become good and sensitive adults, to recognize that they are more fortunate than many. And they are on their way.

My kids watch over me. Having to be concerned for another at a tender age, they have had to abandon the narcissism of youth. That is not all bad. "Be careful, dad," Gabe warns. "Don't trip over those roots." We have wandered off the sidewalk, and he is worried for me. We take our kids and their friends to a movie. The show is in one of New York's vertical multiplex monstrosities. The endless escalator rides carry us high. The crowds are crushing. As each escalator expedition approaches a new floor, Gabe turns and yells through the packed bodies and din, "Be careful dad, we're at the end again. Don't fall."

As with most parents, I used to think only of caring for my own. A young child looking out for a parent seemed to go against the natural order of things. That view has changed. Love from a child plays out with warm, meaningful gestures. My children are learning important lessons about life. That people are not perfect. That some of us need help. These lessons are worthwhile.

I struggle to move beyond the guilt that my children must live with my problems. My kids are wonderful friends, and when they come to my aid, I am getting better at dismissing the remorse I feel about not being able to be the caretaker.

Everyone in the house but the dog is in the act. We stand at the kitchen in our house. "Richard, I'll do that," Meredith says, moving in swiftly after hearing the shattering glass and reaching for a broom. "You can't see well enough." I cringe in silence. We drive down the street. "Why don't you wait in the car," Meredith suggests as she jumps out to finish a few errands I should be sharing. "I will just be a minute." I wait. Ben and I amble through town. "Dad, there's a bench," Ben points out on a local street. Hang out there, okay? The store is a long walk. I will be right back." And I sit.

These are scenes from my life. I am the beleaguered character feeling so small next to the beautiful leading lady who has grown larger than life. Continuous compromise takes a cumulative toll, the body in motion, now at rest and likely to remain so. This is not a sporadic choreography of an occasional bad weekend, a one-time twisted ankle or sore knee. Standing on the sidelines is a way of life. The psychological fallout only adds up and multiplies, weighing heavy.[1]

Discussion Questions

1. To be adaptable means to adjust one's self to circumstances that are new, changing, or less than ideal. What are some statements made by Richard Cohen that describe how he has been able to adapt to life in a body that has been compromised by disease?
2. The quotation of Nietzsche that introduces this story is one that is well known and often quoted. Do you agree with it? Do you know of examples of people made stronger by their undesirable situations? Personally have you been made stronger by a disappointment or misfortune?
3. What do the phrases, "Continuous compromise takes a cumulative toll," and, "Standing on the sidelines is a way of life," tell you about Richard Cohen's understanding of his life?

Suggested Follow-Up

Richard Cohen wrote, "I must rise above the culture of perfection." An indication that ours is a "culture of perfection" is the popularity of cosmetic surgery. A research assignment on cosmetic surgery will serve as a segue to a discussion of a "culture of perfection."

TRAGIC OPTIMISM

*If someone were to ask us the truth of Dostoevski's statement that flatly
defines a man as a being who can get used to anything, we would reply,
"Yes, a man can get used to anything, but do not ask us how."*
                                                              –Viktor Frankl

*Concerning credibility, Elie Wiesel, has said, "It is not what you say, but
who you are when you say it." If Wiesel's observation is correct then
what Viktor Frankl has said is worthy of our attention. Taken from his
life as a respected psychiatrist and relocated to a Nazi concentration
camp, Frankl contemplated the meaning of life amidst unchosen and intolerable circumstances. This essay provides a summary of his thoughts
on life's meaning and teaching on "tragic optimism."*

Viktor Frankl entered Auschwitz hiding a manuscript in the inner
pocket of his coat. "I must keep this manuscript at all costs, "he told a
fellow prisoner, "it contains my life's work."[1] The manuscript did not
survive; Frankl did. Ironically, in nine consecutive days in 1945 he
wrote his memoir, *Man's Search for Meaning*. He wrote it to convey his
story as, "a concrete example that life holds a potential meaning under
any conditions, even the most miserable ones."[2] He wrote that, "One
should not search for an abstract meaning of life."[3] He believed that the
meaning of life differs from day to day and from hour to hour with each
new situation. As each situation presents a challenge to meet or problem
to solve, the question asked of each of us: *What are you going to do in
the present circumstances to bring meaning to your life?*

Essential to Dr. Frankl's philosophy is *tragic optimism*, a term re-
sulting from his combination of the word for *unhappiness brought on
by fate* (tragedy) with the Latin word for *the best* (optimum*). According to Frankl, the three tragedies of life are pain, guilt, and death.
Since they are inevitable, he believes we should use them to our ad-
vantage. To use them in this way is a matter of personal choice and the
only way to bring meaning to our temporary lives that are punctuated
by pain and guilt. He admitted that this choice, "presupposes that life
is potentially meaningful under any conditions, even those which are
most miserable. And this in turn presupposes the human capacity to
creatively turn life's negative aspects into something positive or con-
structive."[4]

Pain

Professor Betty Sue Flowers has written, "Pain is a mechanism for growth; it carves out the heart to make room for compassion."[5] Perhaps life's most painful experience is the death of one's child. Harold Kushner, John Walsh, and Nicholas Wolterstorff each lost a son. Kushner's son, Aaron, died of progeria, a rare genetic disorder characterized by premature aging. Aaron Kushner died of old age at fourteen. Walsh's six-year-old son, Adam, was abducted and murdered. Wolterstorff's son, Eric, fell to his death in a mountain climbing accident.

Reflecting on the death of his son, Rabbi Kushner wrote a book that has provided support for thousands of people: *When Bad Things Happen to Good People*. Wolterstorff's book, *Lament for a Son*, eloquently expresses the thoughts and feelings of those who have lost a child. By expressing his grief, this brilliant philosophy professor has given a voice to parents in mourning. Walsh is the well-known host of the television program, "America's Most Wanted" and was instrumental in the formation of the National Center for Missing and Exploited Children. He is committed to the capture and imprisonment of child abductors.

These men are three examples of pain generating compassion. Each of them chose to redeem his pain by doing something to help others in a similar plight. They teach us that the most effective comforters are *wounded healers*.[6] Frankl is among those who believe that when a person responds to the pain of others it has a palliative effect on one's own:

> The way in which a man accepts his fate and all the suffering
> it entails, the way in which he takes up his cross, gives him
> ample opportunity—even under the most difficult circumstances –
> to add a deeper meaning to his life.[7]

Guilt

In Lucy Maude Montgomery's short story, "The Price," a guilt-ridden woman has determined to miss no opportunity to punish herself for her sin. Christine North believed that her carelessness caused the death of her cousin, Agatha, and resolved, "I have robbed her of life. I will not have life myself."[8] Christine sentenced herself to a life of ever increasing acts of atonement; the more unpleasant, the better. Eventually, her need for self-infliction became an obsession and she decided to adopt a child.

The thought came to her that she would adopt a child. Nothing
would be more distasteful to her. She had always disliked
children. Most of all she disliked ugly children. She went to the
orphan asylum in the city and brought home the ugliest inmate –
a boy of eight with a pitiful little face that had been scarred by
some inhuman attack of a drunken father.[9]

In stark contrast to Christine North's response to her guilt is Frankl's
counsel to, "(derive) from guilt the opportunity to change oneself for
the better."[10] C.S. Lewis reasoned similarly in *The Problem of Pain* in
which he stated that although guilt is not good in and of itself, it could
result in something good."[11] For Frankl, guilt is a tool for self-correc-
tion and improvement. And, like any tool, it should be put away after it
has served its purpose. We experience guilt when we fail to live up to a
standard we have set for ourselves. The antidote for guilt is sincere con-
trition and recommitment to that standard. Jeremiah Denton's memoir,
When Hell Was in Session, recounts his seven years and eight months as
a prisoner of war in Vietnam. After he succumbed to the horrific torture
that accompanied interrogation by giving up information, he recommit-
ted to his goal of not giving his captors what they wanted."[12]

Death

Shortly before his death in the spring of 1995, Brent Foster reflected:

These were supposed to have been the best days of my life.
Instead I am at the losing end of an eight-year battle with
cancer. And although only twenty-one, my body has grown
extremely weak and will soon fail me altogether.[13]

Brent Foster lived well, if not long. A high school valedictorian and the
first Shenandoah (Iowa) High School student to attend Harvard, he
filled his life with every available academic and athletic activity that interested him; even when it meant playing basketball on a prosthetic leg.
He was the embodiment of these words of the philosopher Elton Trueblood:

Each of us is bound to die, and every rational person is highly
conscious that his life is short, but there need be no tragedy in
this. It is surely not so bad to die, providing one has really

lived *before* he dies. Life need not be long to be good, for indeed it cannot be long. The tragedy is not that all die, but that so many fail to really live.[14]

Even for Jeanne Calmunt, the French woman who died in 1998 at age 123, life is brief. Frankl adjures us to be mindful that as we age each remaining day is a greater percentage of the rest of our lives. Rather than lament over the unalterable fact that life is a brief candle, "(derive) from life's transitoriness an incentive to take responsible action."[15] For Frankl, responsible action means making a decision and acting on it in every one of life's innumerable situations. The guiding question for our decisions and actions is: *What can I do in this situation that will bring meaning to it?*

In the movie "Fearless" terrified passengers on an ill-fated airliner face imminent death as their plane is rapidly descending in a nosedive. One man, Max Klein, chooses to spend the last minutes of his life calming and comforting a little boy who is traveling alone. In real life, a pregnant woman, Clementina Geraci, decided to forego the aggressive cancer treatment that might have saved her life but was likely to induce an abortion. Both of these decisions serve as illustrations of responsible action in the face of impending death. Trueblood and Frankl would remind us that death is impending for all of us.

Conclusion

Over seventy years ago another psychiatrist, Carl Jung, contemplated the meaning of life and wrote: "Among my patients from many countries, there is a considerable number who came to see me, not because they were suffering from a neurosis, but because they could find no meaning in life."[16] When Viktor Frankl was asked how he felt about his book's status as a bestseller (it's been translated into twenty languages and sold over two million copies in the English version) he responded: "If hundreds of thousands of people reach out for a book whose very title promises to deal with the question of a meaning to life, it must be a question that burns under their fingernails."[17]

Discussion Questions

1. Do you believe that a person can live a good life without wrestling with the question: *What is the meaning of life?*

2. Have you ever read a book, seen a movie, heard a sermon, or, in some other way, had your attention directed to the question of life's meaning?

3. Shakespeare's Macbeth says, "Life is walking shadow, a poor player who struts and frets his hour upon the stage and then is heard no more. It is a tale told by an idiot, full of sound and fury, signifying nothing." Contrast these words with Dr. Frankl's *tragic optimism*.

4. Do you believe that religion has anything to contribute to the discussion of the meaning of life?

Suggested Follow-Up

1. Show the well-known *carpe diem* scene from the movie "Dead Poets Society" in which an English teacher played by Robin Williams creatively pursues with his students the question of life's meaning. This scene is approximately five minutes in length and contained in the first half-hour of the movie. It was produced by Touchstone Home Video and its running time is 128 minutes.

2. Assign an analytical essay in which students are asked to interpret and apply the colloquialism: *You have to play the hand you've been dealt.*

ABRAHAM LINCOLN'S DEPRESSION

I am the most miserable man living. If what I feel were equally distributed to the whole human family, there would not be one cheerful face on earth. Whether I shall ever be better, I cannot tell; I awfully forebode I shall not. To remain as I am is impossible; I must die or be better, it appears to me."

–Abraham Lincoln (January 23, 1841 letter to his law partner William Herndon)

In a recently published book about Abraham Lincoln are these words: "When faced with uncertainty he had the patience, endurance, and vigor to stay in that place of tension, and the courage to be alone."[1] The following essay focuses on Lincoln's depression and his extraordinary determination to meet his responsibilities in spite of it.

In the psychiatric literature depression is categorized as a mood disorder and defined as a "pattern of sadness, anxiety, fatigue, agitated behavior, and reduced ability to function and interact with others."[2] The brilliant and chronically depressed writer William Styron chafes at the use of the word *depression* to designate the condition that plagues him. He considers it "a true wimp of a word for such a major illness."[3]

Adaptability is the capacity to adjust oneself to new or changed circumstances. While President, Abraham Lincoln's circumstances included a profound and unremitting depression intensified by the death of his eleven-year-old son, Willie, and the war that threatened to dissemble the nation. For human beings, adaptability is not a thoughtless, Darwinian process of transgenerational mutations, but a conscious determination to accommodate to the reality of circumstances and persevere. People choose to adapt.

Adaptability results from the decision that something is more important than the relief that would come from withdrawing from a responsibility or quitting altogether. It is similar to courage, which is the decision that something is more important than comfort or safety. Both adaptability and courage require a determination to persevere. Adaptability, courage, and perseverance are virtues because they are demonstrations of people continuing to demand much of themselves while their strength is being eroded. The poet Rudyard Kipling recognized this and wrote, "If you can force your heart and nerve and sinew to serve their purpose long after they are gone ... you'll be a man my son."[4]

Lincoln's greatness does not reside in overcoming depression and then going on to do great work. Instead, he triumphed over his depression by not allowing it to prevent him from doing his duty. He believed that, "he had been charged with so vast and sacred a trust that he felt he had no moral right to shrink" from his responsibilities."[5] Although Lincoln's theology is not altogether clear, there is no mistaking that he carried on his work with a sense of calling; a determination to accomplish something while he lived; and to have his name connected "with the great events of his generation."[6] He certainly fulfilled this calling.

One hundred-and-forty years after Lincoln's death at least three new books about different aspects of his life have appeared, two of which have risen to *New York Times* bestseller's status. This man, who often wept in public and alarmed his friends with talk of suicide, adapted and persevered. On April 14th, 1865, John Wilkes Booth assassinated Abraham Lincoln. It is conceivable that one of the most notorious crimes in American history was an act of unintended benevolence by which one man unburdened another of intolerable suffering.

Discussion Questions

1. Even among those who do not know about Lincoln's depression are many who consider him one of America's greatest Presidents. Why is he so highly regarded as a President of the United States?
2. From either reading or experience, what do you know about depression? Do you believe it is an actual psychological condition (i.e. mental illness)?
3. Can you think of other examples of adaptability that you admire?

Suggested Follow-Up

1. Invite a mental health professional to speak to your class about depression.
2. Assign and discuss William Styron's 1990 bestseller *Darkness Visible*. This brief (less than 100 pages) memoir is a moving and superbly written account of the author's depression.
3. Assign and discuss the Gettysburg Address. In the discussion, pursue the questions: Why is this one of the most famous speeches in American history? What does this speech imply about Abraham Lincoln himself?

Chapter II

Altruism

THREE CASES OF SELF-SACRIFICE

The man who has made a sacrifice of himself lives entirely for the happiness of others, finding his own felicity in the felicity of the public.
                                                                  –Darren M. McMahon

Altruism, or benevolence, is the consideration of others before oneself. It is the opposite of egoism, the quality of thinking or acting with only oneself and one's own interests in mind. The following are three demonstrations of altruism.

In his book, *The Pursuit of Happiness*, psychologist David Myers provides the following narrative.

With Nazi submarines sinking ships faster than the Allied forces could replace them, the troop ship *SS Dorchester* steamed out of New York harbor with 904 men headed for Greenland. Among those leaving anxious families behind were four chaplains, Methodist preacher George Fox, Rabbi Alexander Goode, Catholic priest John Washington, and Reformed Church minister Clark Polling. Some 150 miles from their destination, a U-456 caught the *Dorchester* in its cross hairs. Within moments of a torpedo's impact, reports Lawrence Elliot, stunned men were pouring out from their bunks as the ship began listing. With power cut off, the escort vessels, unaware of the unfolding tragedy, pushed on in the

darkness. On board, chaos reigned as panicky men came up from
the hold without life jackets and leaped into overcrowded lifeboats.
    When the four chaplains made it up to the steeply sloping deck,
they began guiding the men to their boat stations. They opened a
storage locker, distributed life jackets, and coaxed the men over the
side. In the icy, oily smeared water, Private William Bednar heard the
chaplains preaching courage and found the strength to swim until he
reached a life raft. Still on board, Grady Clark watched in awe as the
chaplains handed out the last life jacket, and then, with ultimate
selflessness, gave away their own. As Clark slipped into the waters
he saw the chaplains standing—their arms linked—praying, in Latin,
Hebrew, and English. Other men, now serene, joined them in a huddle
as the *Dorchester* slid beneath the sea.[1]

Under the headline, "Mother picks death to continue her life through
son's birth," *The Washington Post* provided the story of a mother who
chose to forego the aggressive cancer treatment that would have aborted
her baby.

> Clementina Geraci, three months pregnant, made the decision of
> her life when doctors told her last spring that her breast cancer had
> spread. She could fight the cancer aggressively and have an abortion,
> or she could take less hazardous cancer drugs and carry the baby to
> term. ... Geraci, known as Tina, died Monday, March 6, at
> Washington Hospital Center, where she had worked as a resident
> in obstetrics and gynecology. She was 34.[2]

A doctor herself, Mrs. Geraci fully understood her treatment options
and the inherent risk in the choice she had made.

> During most of her pregnancy, Geraci took taxol, which doctors
> thought would not harm Dylan (her son). She had to stop taking the
> drug during the seventh month of her pregnancy, and Dylan was born
> one month prematurely by a Caesarean section, during which doctors
> discovered cancer in her liver. She resumed treatment, but it was too late.[3]

In another news story, the *New York Times News Service* reported that
a man who had donated one kidney had his wife in a dither over his determination to donate his remaining kidney.

> Having already given one kidney to a total stranger, Zell Kravinsky
> was ... making a case for giving away his other one. "What if

someone needed it who could produce more good than me?" Kravinsky said on Tuesday in an interview. "What if I was a perfect match for a dying scientist who was the intellectual driving force behind a breakthrough cure for cancer or AIDS or on the brink of unlocking the secrets of cell regeneration?"

The consequences of Kravinsky giving away his other kidney are apparent—he would die. ... Talking to Kravinsky, 48, is unsettling. His brand of altruism borders on obsession, perhaps even a sort of benign madness, although he was subjected to a battery of psychiatric tests before the hospital would accept him as a kidney donor. ...

His wife, Emily, a psychiatrist, has threatened to divorce him, Kravinsky said, worried that his altruism is coming at the expense of their four children. The Kravinsky's have given away $15 million, with Zell Kravinsky promising to give away virtually everything the family has. ...

Kravinsky says he is only applying the principle of "maximum human utility," explaining, "My life is not worth more than anyone else's." ...

"No one should have a vacation home until everyone has a place to live" he said. "No one should have a second car until everyone has one. And no one should have two kidneys until everyone has one."[4]

Discussion Questions

1. Are there any differences in your thoughts and feelings concerning these stories of altruism? If so, how do you account for these differences?
2. Is Zell Kravinsky a man of unsound mind who is incapable of exercising sound judgment? If so, what is it about his thinking that marks him as a man who is insane?
3. Concerning suicide, psychiatrist Thomas Szasz has written, "He who does not accept and respect those who want to reject life does not truly accept and respect life itself."[5] Does Dr. Szasz's opinion concerning suicide also apply to the acts of altruism demonstrated by the four chaplains, Clementina Geraci, and Zell Kravinsky?

Suggested Follow-Up

1. Assign an essay in which students are required to describe an act they consider altruistic. Their selection may come from real life, literature, or the theatre.

2. The philosopher Ayn Rand defined selfishness as "carefully considered self-interest" and considered it a virtue. She rejected altruism as ethical, considering it "self-sacrifice" and "slavery."[6] Assign an investigation of Ayn Rand's thoughts on the subjects of altruism and selfishness.

INTO THE SUN (KAY REDFIELD JAMISON)

A man has made at least a start on discovering the meaning of life when he plants shade trees under which he knows full well he will never sit.
　　　　　　　　　　　　　　　　　　　　　　　　–Elton Trueblood

Kay Redfield Jamison is a psychologist and Professor of Psychiatry at the Johns Hopkins University School of Medicine. "Into the Sun" is the story that begins her bestselling memoir, An Unquiet Mind: A Memoir of Moods and Madness, *in which she reveals that she has bi-polar disorder (also known as manic-depression). Perhaps she chose this narrative to begin her book because it describes a heroic, altruistic act that prevented her life from ending at age seven.*

I was standing with my head back, one pigtail caught between my teeth, listening to the jet overhead. The noise was loud, unusually so, which meant that it was close. My elementary school was near Andrews Air Force Base, just out side Washington; many of us were pilots kids, so the sound was a matter of routine. Being routine, however, didn't take away from the magic, and I instinctively looked up from the playground to wave. I knew, of course, that the pilot couldn't see me—I always knew that—just as I knew that even if he could see me the odds were that it wasn't actually my father. But it was one of those things one did, and anyway, I loved any and all excuses just to stare up into the skies. My father, a career Air Force officer, was first and foremost a scientist and only secondarily a pilot. But he loved to fly, and, because he was a meteorologist, both his mind and his soul ended up being in the skies. Like my father, I looked up rather more than I looked out.

When I would say to him that the Navy and the Army were so much *older* than the Air Force, had so much more tradition and legend, he would say, Yes, that's true, but the Air Force is the *future*. Then he would always add: And—we can fly. This statement of creed would usually be followed by an enthusiastic rendering of the Air Force song, fragments of which remain with me to this day, nested together somewhat improbably, with phrases from Christmas cards , early poems, and bits and pieces from the Book of Common Prayer: all having great mood and meaning from childhood, and still retaining the power to quicken the pulses.

So I would listen and believe and, when I would hear the words "Off we go into the wild blue yonder," I would think that "wild" and "yonder" were among the most wonderful words I had ever heard; likewise I would feel the total exhilaration of the phrase "Climbing high into the sun" and know instinctively that I was a part of those who loved the vastness of the sky.

The noise of the jet became louder, and I saw the other children in my second-grade class suddenly dart their heads upward. The plane was coming in very low, then it streaked past us, scarcely missing the playground. As we stood there clumped together and absolutely terrified, it flew into the trees, exploding directly in front of us. The ferocity of the crash could be felt and heard in the plane's awful impact; it also could be seen in the frightening but terrible lingering loveliness of the flames that followed. Within minutes, it seemed, mothers were pouring onto the playground to reassure children that it was not their fathers; fortunately for my brother and sister and myself it was not ours either. Over the next few days it became clear from the release of the young pilot's final message to the control tower before he died, that he knew he could save his own life by bailing out. He also knew, however, that by doing so he risked that his unaccompanied plane would fall onto the playground and kill those of us who were there.

The dead pilot became a hero, transformed into a scorchingly vivid, completely impossible ideal for what was meant by the concept of duty. It was an impossible ideal, but all the more compelling and haunting because of its very unobtainability. The memory of the crash came back to me many times over the years, as a reminder both of how one aspires after and needs such ideals, and how killingly difficult it is to achieve them. I never again looked at the sky and saw only vastness and beauty, From that afternoon on I saw that death was also and always there.[1]

Discussion Questions

1. For Dr. Jamison the dead pilot became the "ideal for what was meant by the concept of duty. She wrote, "The memory of the crash came back to me many times over the years, as a reminder both of how one aspires after and needs such ideals, and how killingly difficult it is to achieve them." An ideal is a perfect model of something. Do you agree with her that we need ideals? If so, why?

2. In addition to the pilot's courage and sense of duty probably having saved her life, why do you think the memory of the crash has come back to her many times over the years?

3. Dr. Phil McGraw, the famous television psychologist, in his book, *Self Matters*, states that our lives are impacted by pivotal people and decisive moments. Pivotal people are those who have affected our lives in a significant and enduring way. Decisive moments are definite points in time when we learned a truth about life that has influenced our thinking ever since. For Kay Jamison the pilot is a pivotal person and the crash a decisive moment. Can you think of a pivotal person and/or decisive moment in your life?

4. The Catholic priest and monastic Thomas Merton wrote, "The first human act is the recognition of how much I owe everybody else."[2] In his book, *Happiness Is a Serious Problem*, Dennis Prager emphasizes that living with a sense of gratitude is necessary for happiness. Do you perceive Dr. Jamison's gratitude in her story? If so, why, since the word, *gratitude*, appears nowhere in the narrative?

Suggested Follow Up

Assign an essay in which students are asked to respond to the following question: Can you think of any time when you have witnessed, benefited from, or demonstrated an act of altruism?

Chapter III

Authenticity

WHAT DOES IT MEAN TO BE REAL?

This above all - to thine own self be true
And it must follow, as the night the day,
Thou canst not then be false to any man.

–Polonius, Hamlet, 1.3.75

Sincerely is a word commonly used in concluding a letter and means to be free from pretense or deceit. It provides reassurance that the correspondence is authentic and can be accepted as trustworthy. What does it mean for a person to be authentic? Using illustrations from literature, this essay attempts to answer this question.

A well-known book among psychiatrists and psychologists is Dr. Milton Rokeach's *The Three Christs of Ypsilanti*.[1] It describes his two-year study of three men in a Michigan mental hospital who had the same psychotic delusion: each believed himself to be Jesus Christ. These patients provide an exotic example of inauthenticity. In contrast to them, an authentic person's real identity, self-concept, and public presentation are in agreement. Each of these three Christs of Ypsilanti had agreement between his self-concept and public presentation, but both were in discord with his real identity.

Authentic people's ideas of themselves (self-concept) are consistent with the facts about them (real identity) as well as the way in which they present themselves to others (public presentation). Knowing one's self is no easy matter. Nietzsche wrote, "We are unknown, we knowers, to ourselves ... we understand ourselves not, in ourselves we are bound to be mistaken...as far as ourselves are concerned we are not knowers."[2] Writer Walter Percy suggested that this unknowingness also applies to one's physical appearance: "Why is it that when you are shown a group photograph in which you are present, you always (and probably covertly) seek yourself out? To see what you look like? Don't you know what you look like?"[3]

Psychologist Erik Erikson coined the term *identity crisis* to characterize the life stage at which the question, "Who am I?" is considered. Typically, but not always, occurring in adolescence, it is the time at which people establish their own values and priorities. A longer form of this question is, "Separately and distinctly from my parents, who am I?" With the answer to this question comes the establishment of identity and the challenge to live authentically. To live authentically is to live in accordance with one's stated values and moral code.

Nathaniel Hawthorne's *The Scarlet Letter* provides a study in contrast between Hester Prynne and Reverend Dimmesdale. Set in Puritan New England, it is the story of a woman whose extramarital affair results in an illegitimate child and the public scorn that went with adultery. Taking responsibility for her sin, Hester carries herself with dignity, raising her child and never disclosing the identity of her lover. Her lover was Reverend Dimmesdale, the community's respected spiritual leader. The minister lives out his years maintaining his image as a man of God. His inauthentic life, known only to him and Hester, is described by Hawthorne with these words:

> It is the unspeakable misery of a life so false as his, that it
> steals the pith and substance out of whatever realities there
> are around us, and which were meant by Heaven to be the
> spirit's joy and nutriment. To the untrue man, the whole
> universe is false—it is impalpable—it shrinks to nothing
> within his grasp. And he himself, in so far as he shows
> himself in a false light, becomes a shadow, or, indeed,
> ceases to exist.[4]

Reverend Dimmesdale's simulation of virtue and godliness qualifies him as a hypocrite. The word *hypocrite* is derived from the Greek word for "actor". (In the theater of ancient Greece, stage performers delivered their lines holding masks that identified the roles they played. The Greek word from which hypocrite is derived literally means "one who speaks from behind a mask.")

People resort to hypocrisy out of fear. It is the fear of humiliation and/or rejection that drives hypocrisy. The hypocrite believes, "If I present myself as I really am, I will not be respected, admired, or loved." To express this in another way, people live inauthentically because they are afraid of the consequences of an authentic life. People who live authentically have congruency in their real selves, self-concepts, and public selves. The wholeness that results from this consistency brings an inner-peace that prevails over fear.

In Margery Williams' children's story *The Velveteen Rabbit*, the skin horse and velveteen rabbit discuss what it means to be real:

The Skin Horse had lived longer in the nursery than any of the others. He was so old that his brown coat was bald in patches and showed the seams underneath, and most of the hairs in his tail had been pulled out to string bead necklaces. He was wise, for he had seen a long succession of mechanical toys arrive to boast and swagger, and by-and-by break their mainsprings and pass away, and he knew that they were only toys, and would never turn into anything else. For nursery magic is very strange and wonderful, and only those playthings that are old and wise and experienced like the Skin Horse understand all about it.

"What is REAL?" asked the Rabbit one day, when they were lying side by side near the nursery fender, before Nana came to tidy the room. "Does it mean having things that buzz inside you and a stick-out handle?"

"Real isn't how you are made," said the Skin Horse. "It's a thing that happens to you. When a child loves you for a long, long time, not just to play with, but REALLY loves you, then you become Real."

"Does it hurt?" asked the Rabbit.

"Sometimes," said the Skin Horse, for he was always truthful. "When you are Real you don't mind being hurt."

"Does it happen all at once, like being wound up," he asked, "or bit by bit?"

"It doesn't happen all at once," said the Skin Horse. "You become. It takes a long time. That's why it doesn't happen often to people who break easily, or have sharp edges, or who have to be carefully kept. Generally, by the time you are Real, most of your hair has been loved off, and your eyes drop out and you get loose in the joints and very shabby. But these things don't matter at all, because once you are Real you can't be ugly, except to people who don't understand."

"I suppose *you* are real?" said the Rabbit. And then he wished he had not said it, for he thought the Skin Horse might be sensitive. But the Skin Horse only smiled.

"The Boy's Uncle made me Real," he said. "That was a great many years ago; but once you are Real you can't become unreal again. It lasts for always."

The Rabbit sighed. He thought it would be a long time before this magic called Real happened to him. He longed to become Real, to know what it felt like; and yet the idea of growing shabby and losing his eyes and whiskers was rather sad. He wished that he could become it without these uncomfortable things happening to him.[5]

The teaching of the skin horse is that being loved, really loved, is a liberating experience. People who are loved unconditionally are able to relax from pretense and live authentically. They are unashamed of and unconcerned with their imperfections, realizing they can't be ugly, "except to people who don't understand."

In *The Search for the Real Self* psychiatrist James Masterson wrote: "The real self allows a person to recognize within herself that special 'someone' who persists through space and time, who endures as a unique entity regardless of how the various parts of it shift and change."[6] If Dr. Masterson and the Skin Horse are correct in their observations about *real* then it is easy to understand why the late Christopher Reeve chose as the title of his memoir *Still Me*.

Discussion Questions

1. Do you agree with Nietzsche's analysis: " … as far as ourselves are concerned we are not knowers"? How is it possible for people to not know themselves?

2. Walker Percy accused us of seeking out ourselves when looking at group pictures that include us. Do you think this is a false accusation? If you agree with him, why do you think people seek out themselves in this way?

3. It is not unusual to hear someone say, "At least I'm not a hypocrite!" Hypocrisy seems to be the one fault people strongly resist admitting. Why do people rarely admit to hypocritical behavior? Do you think it is possible to be hypocritical without realizing it? (Or, do people always know when they are being hypocritical?)

Suggested Follow-Up

Convergent data is information that is identical and gathered from several sources that are independent of each other. Convergent data is one of the surest ways of learning about our real selves. Instruct students to list three to five personality traits they have been told they have by people who have not consulted with each other. The traits can be positive or negative. After compiling the list, further instruct the students to consider whether or not they agree with their convergent data about themselves.

Chapter IV

Compassion

ILLYSSA (TIM GREEN)

Always be a little kinder than necessary.
–Sir James Matthew Barrie

Compassionate people recognize and respond to the troubles of others. Tim Green is a remarkably versatile individual. An All-American football player at Syracuse University, he went on to a career in the National Football League with the Atlanta Falcons. Now retired from football, he is a lawyer, bestselling author, and television sports analyst. It is difficult to imagine Tim Green having benefited from someone intervening on his behalf. In this story he benefits from the compassion of his then future wife, Illyssa.

She was nice to everyone who crossed her path. Although she'd grown up in a world of limousines and servants, Illyssa treated the woman who cleaned the hotel or the guy who pumped the gas into the car with the same dignity she afforded the owner of the team when she met him at a barbecue. It was fascinating to me to see a woman who came from the upper class act as if there were no such thing. Everyone to her was a person. She seemed as impervious to the grease under some person's fingernails as to the diamonds around the neck of another.

At the same time, she was no pushover. Far from that. While she'd sit demurely at a restaurant, effortlessly using the most proper manners, if someone crossed Illyssa, they knew about it. At an expensive French restaurant one night, the maitre d'; who had a marvelous accent, told us we'd have to wait quite a while. He also got huffy with me because I had a shirt with no collar under my jacket. I was red-faced and ready to walk out with my tail between my legs when Illyssa stopped me with a firm grip on my arm.

"You're not an owner are you?" She said pleasantly to the snooty maitre d'.

"Pardon *me* mademoiselle?" He said, obviously affronted.

"I know you're not the owner," she said, staring him down, "because someone who owns a restaurant would never treat someone like that."

"I simply referred to monsieur's choice of clothing," he sniffed. "This is a very fine restaurant."

"I'll tell the owner you said that," Illyssa said flatly. "Where is he? I want to speak with him."

"Monsieur Voltaire is not here tonight," he said, beginning to look rather uncomfortable.

"I would like his phone number then," she said. "I think I should speak to him. If I had a restaurant, I would want to know if one of my employees were treating customers the way you do."

"Ha!" The man scoffed, trying to play the whole thing off as a joke, but quite aware that she meant business.

"Maybe you should show us to a table by the window," Illyssa said pleasantly. "Right away."

"Of course, mademoiselle," he said politely, with a smile no less.

After we were seated, the waiter informed us that Monsieur Maitre d' would like to buy us a bottle of wine.

When we were alone, I whispered, "That was cool."

Illyssa treated the whole thing with nonchalance, but did explain gently, "You don't ever have to let someone treat you like that."

"This is a fancy place, though," I said in defense of my tormentor. "I should have worn a tie. You told me to wear a tie."

"I didn't tell you you should," She reminded me. "I said you might want to. That you didn't is perfectly fine. Don't worry about that. And this place isn't so fancy. That guy's not even French."

"How do you know that?" I said, mystified.

"I just know." She said with a shrug.

When I used the bathroom later that night, the attendant confirmed for me that, in fact, the maitre d' was from New Jersey.

How could I not be in love with a girl like that? She was the perfect paradox: demure but bold, soft but strong, quiet but opinionated, confident but humble, passionate but prudish. I thought Illyssa Wolkoff was the most beautiful human being ever to walk the earth. I was still intent on finding my mother and succeeding in the NFL, but my consciousness seemed to have suddenly sponged up some liquid calm. If all else failed me, there was someone of great substance and attractiveness who cared about me and loved me, maybe even adored me, no matter what had come before.[1]

Discussion Questions

1. The story begins with, "She was nice to everyone who crossed her path." Do you think Illyssa was nice to the Maitre d'? If you think she was not nice to him, what word describes how she treated him?
2. What do you infer from the Maitre d' offering to buy Tim and Illyssa a bottle of wine? If you were in their situation, would you have accepted it? Why or why not?
3. What do you think made Illyssa confident in her deduction that the Maitre d' was not the owner of the restaurant?
4. Have you ever been treated disrespectfully as a customer in a restaurant, store, or other place of business? If so, did you address the treatment you received? If you did address the treatment, do you have any regrets about how you responded?
5. Illyssa said to Tim, "You don't ever have to let someone treat you like that." Is she implying that Tim should treat people the same way they treat him. Do you think she is criticizing Tim for not standing up for himself?

Suggested Follow-Up

This story is from Tim Green's book, *A Man and His Mother: An Adopted Son's Search*. His biological mother gave him up for adoption at birth and as an adult he searched for her. It is a well-written, interesting story of an extraordinarily accomplished man who lived for many years with a nagging curiosity about why his birth mother decided not to raise him.

A CHILD SHALL LEAD THEM
(DALE HANSEN BOURKE)

The wolf will live with the lamb ... and a child shall lead them.
                                                  –Isaiah 11:6

This is a kleenex story in which a little boy obliviously plays a starring role in a sacred drama. There are at least two surprises in this story written by the boy's mother, Dale Hansen Bourke. One is the little boy's radical act of kindness. The other is the effect of this act on a cantankerous, bigoted man.

The sun was just coming up as we entered Los Angeles International Airport. I was carrying a small suitcase, and my young son wore a toy-filled backpack decorated with ducks. We were headed home after a week in California.

We're beginning to get the hang of this, I thought a bit smugly as Chase and I wound our way through the airport and into the check-in line. Since my son's birth, we had traveled together whenever possible. At times the logistics seemed overwhelming; changing diapers, warming bottles, and amusing an active two-year-old within the confines of an airplane could be a monumental task.

But right from the start, Chase loved the adventure of it all, and now we negotiated airports together like pros.

"I'm sorry, ma'am, but the flight has been cancelled," the man said as he took our tickets. "However, I can put you on our next flight to Denver that leaves in two hours. Then you can change planes in Chicago..."

As the ticket agent explained the new route that would zigzag us across the country over the next twelve hours, I looked at my son and felt my confidence dissolve. "There's got to be something else," I said urgently. "Doesn't any other airline fly to Washington?"

"Well," the man said, after staring at his computer for several minutes, "our competition has a nonstop flight leaving in the next hour, but you'd have to go all the way to the last terminal. I don't think you can make it in time."

"Could you please book us on it?" Barely waiting for his nod, I gathered up our belongings, and we took off running.

After a mad dash, we made it to the other terminal. But when I presented our tickets again, explaining we had been rescheduled on the new flight, the reservationist apologized, "I'm sorry, but we don't have any reservations for you. The agent at the other airline must not have called them in."

I must have looked like I was about to cry because the woman gave me an encouraging smile and added, "Let's see what we can do."

The flight was already full, but we waited and she punched buttons, two seats miraculously opened.

"We got you on!" she said excitedly. "But you'll have to hurry. The flight's about to leave."

Thanking her, we rushed down the long hall to our airplane. At last we spotted our gate and the blinking light indicating the plane was already boarding. We rushed ahead only to be stopped by a group of people wearing tattered clothes, huddled in the boarding area. They didn't seem to be moving toward the airplane.

"Excuse me," I said.

"'scuse me," Chase mimicked.

But neither of our requests received attention from the group. Finally, a woman from the airline herded the group to the side and motioned for us to pass. "They're from Cambodia," she explained. "They don't speak English."

As we passed the group, I noticed that despite the California heat, they all wore heavy coats. Still, they seemed to huddle together as if for warmth.

We walked on to the airplane and made our way to the back, finding our seats in the middle of the smoking section. "Oh great. We're stuck behind a kid," the man behind me said to his wife. I resisted the urge to give him a dirty look and concentrated instead on getting Chase settled in his seat.

Just as we fastened our seat belts, the group of people we had seen earlier were escorted down the aisle.

The flight attendant pointed them toward seats across from ours. As they sat down, I realized that they were part of an extended family: mother, father, two boys, and their grandmother.

They seemed nervous and tired, and they sat in their seats without removing their coats or storing the shopping bags each carried. I realized then that all their possessions were either in their bags or on their back, and they were afraid to part with anything.

My attention turned back to my son as he proclaimed, "Look, Mommy, a movie," pointing at the safety film that was playing on the airplane's screen.

"Let's talk quietly," I urged, not wanting to give the man behind me any more reason to dislike children.

"Okay," Chase whispered, then in total delight shrieked, "A teddy bear! That boy in the movie has a teddy bear!" Sure enough, my eagle-eyed son had spotted the one toy in the entire safety film and wanted everyone to share his discovery.

I heard the man behind me swear about children and "smelly foreigners," and I bit my lip as I thought of all the people in the world who must offend him.

Take-off occupied our attention for the next few minutes. As soon as the seat belt light went off, Chase was ready to empty his backpack and begin playing with his toys. "My train. Where's my train?" he asked, panic creeping into his voice. His little plastic train had become his favorite possession over the past weeks, whenever it was out of sight for more than a few minutes he became frantic. He even slept with it in his crib.

But his trains were safely packed away in my purse along with our tickets, and Chase squealed again as he saw them. We played with the trains and his other toys for the next hour, trying to ignore the smoke that surrounded us and the ever-grumbling man behind me. I looked up and saw two pairs of big brown eyes watching Chase play with his toys. I realized the two little boys had sat quietly for the past hour without anything to amuse them. I thought of the four hours left in their long journey, and my heart went out to the young boys, one my son's age and the other a little older.

"Chase," I said, "those little boys don't have any toys and you have so many."

"Their toys are in their suitcase," he said matter-of-factly.

"No," I explained, "they don't have toys at all." Chase looked at me skeptically.

"Not even at home?" he asked, beginning to understand the seriousness of the situation. Chase was good about sharing toys with his playmates, but he lived in a world of privileged children. So the thought of no toys—not even at home—was new to Chase.

"Maybe you could let the boys play with some of your toys," I nudged.

At first Chase pretended not the hear me, but I knew it was his way of thinking through a decision. "All right, Mommy," he said, less than enthusiastically. Then looking at me with wide eyes, he asked, "Do I have to let them play with my train?"

"No, Chase," I assured him. Relieved, he carefully picked out two Matchbox race cars, marched across the airplane aisle, and ceremoniously presented each car to the little boys who looked surprised and then thrilled. The boys' mother looked at me with a grateful smile, the grandmother patted Chase on the head, and the little boys grinned and bobbed their heads up and down to show their thanks for the cars they were holding carefully.

My own son turned and looked at me with a big smile. "They like them, Mommy," he said excitedly. Then soberly, "They don't have *any* toys, not even at home." And after glancing at them one more time, he looked at me and said, "They can have my train too."

I watched with tears in my eyes as my son took his cherished train and handed it to the two boys, who seemed to understand the value of the gift. From behind me, I heard the familiar gruff voice say, "You've got a fine little boy there." I smiled at the man, then leaned over to give my son a hug. He struggled out of my arms and back to his toys, oblivious to the sacred drama in which he had just played a starring role.

The rest of the flight went quickly. I watched Chase play, and silently thanked God for the cancellations and confusion that had led us to two seats in the middle of the smoking section on a crowded airplane.

"*A little child shall lead them.*" As these words ran through my mind, I realized that God could use one small gesture to welcome a family of pilgrims, open the eyes of a bigot, and teach a sometimes smug mother that only He is truly in control.[1]

Discussion Questions

1. Chase's mother made the following observation about the irascible man: "I bit my lip as I thought of all the people in the world who must offend him." What do you think of her observation? What does her observation imply about her?
2. The man in the story said to Chase's mother, "You've got a fine little boy there." What do his words imply about him?

3. What is it about giving away his train that makes Chase's act an act of extraordinary kindness? Have you ever personally experienced a similar act of kindness?
4. Psychologists speak of *nature and nurture* when discussing the development of personality, an individual's characteristic pattern of thinking, feeling, acting, and relating. Do you think Chase's compassion is a result of the way he was born (*nature*) or raised (*nurture*)?

Suggested Follow-Up

1. "Searching for Bobby Fischer" is an award winning film (1994 Parent's Choice Award) about a seven-year-old chess prodigy who, like Chase, is uncommonly kind. It is a movie with an excellent cast that includes Laurence Fishburne, Ben Kingsley, and Joe Mantegna.
2. A discussion of compassion and kindness should include giving in an unhealthy way and the importance of boundaries. Dr. Seuss' *Thidwick, the Big-Hearted Moose* is the story of a well-intentioned moose whose kindness is misguided.

Chapter V

Courage

HEROIC ACTS

What makes a king out of a slave? Courage! What makes the flag on the mast to wave? Courage! What makes the elephant charge his tusk, in the misty mist or the dusky dusk? What makes the muskrat guard his musk? Courage! What makes the sphinx the seventh wonder? Courage! What makes the dawn come up like thunder? Courage! What makes the Hottentot so hot? What puts the "ape" in apricot? What have they got that I ain't got? Courage!
—The Cowardly Lion (*The Wizard of Oz*)

Courage doesn't always roar. Sometimes courage is the quiet voice at the end of the day saying, "I will try again tomorrow."
—Mary Anne Radmacher

What is courage and why is it universally recognized as a virtue? A dictionary definition of courage is, "the attitude of facing and dealing with anything recognized as dangerous, difficult, or painful, instead of withdrawing from it."[1] *In the same dictionary a coward is defined as, "one who is unable to control his fear and so shrinks from danger and trouble."*[2] *Philosopher Elton Trueblood has written, "When ancient Greek thinking analyzed human conduct ... they finally arrived at substantial agreement that the ultimate virtues were four: wisdom, courage, temperance and justice."*[3] *He also referred to courage as "outstanding boldness"and wrote that the great majority of men and women who have lived well have been people of valor."*[4]

31

The actions of Gregory Ysais and Lenny Skutnik described in this es-
say are offered as illustrations of courage. However, since neither ad-
mitted to fear, it could be argued that their life-saving deeds were not
courageous. Can a person show bravery without experiencing fear?
This is one of the questions that arises when considering courage.

In his book, *Everyday Morality*, Professor Mike W. Martin describes
a terrifying experience.

In a wilderness area in a city where I live, a woman was
hiking with her five-year-old daughter in 1986. A mountain
lion attacked the girl and dragged her into some bushes.
The mother's frantic screams were heard by Gregory Ysais,
a thirty-six-year-old electronics technician who happened to be
hiking in the same area. Without any hesitation Ysais ran to the
scene to find the cougar gripping the bloody and squirming child
by the back of her neck. Ysais grabbed a branch and repeatedly
swung it over the cougar's head. The full-grown cougar responded
with threatening roars and quick strikes with his huge paws.
After a few minutes the cougar dropped the child long enough for
her to be pulled away.
Ysais later reported that he had never been in a life-and-death
situation before and had never thought of himself as a hero: "I
didn't give it much thought. I just heard people crying for help,
and I just ran as fast as I could. I was just doing what I had to do.
I couldn't think of anything else."[5]

Four years earlier, a man responded similarly when Air Florida Flight
90 failed to clear the 14th Street Bridge in Washington, DC. Until he
dove into the icy water of the Potomac River, Lenny Skutnik was one
of hundreds of bystanders watching the horrific scene. He rescued
Priscilla Tirado, whose husband and son were among the seventy-eight
passengers killed in the crash. Skutnik swam out to her when he realized she was too weak to grasp the rescue rings that had been lowered
from a helicopter.

President Reagan spoke of Skutnik's bravery with these words:
"Nothing had picked him out particularly to be a hero, but without hesitation there he was and he saved her life."[6] When interviewed, Skutnik
depreciated his heroic act. "I just did it. When I got out of the water, I
was satisfied. I did what I set out to do."[7]

In *Virtues and Vices*, James Wallace provides six criteria for courageous acts. For an act to be courageous there must be the recognition of danger, estimation of risk, an option of not acting, consensus of danger (i.e. most people would recognize the act as dangerous), absence of coercion (i.e. no fear of a greater punishment for not acting), and soundness of mind (i.e. the individual's self-control is not impaired by insanity or substance abuse).[8]

Aristotle defined a courageous act as one in which there is a balance between recklessness and cowardice. He believed that a rash person neither recognizes danger nor experiences fear while a coward is immobilized by fear. Aristotle implied that fear is a necessary part of a courageous act. When reflecting on Gregory Ysais, Professor Martin noted Ysais' absence of fear and still considered his intervention an act of courage. For Martin, courage is shown when action is taken in situations generally regarded as dangerous, even if fear did not have to be overcome.

If fear must be overcome for an act to be considered courageous, then neither Ysais nor Skutnik acted bravely. Yet, how many people would have fought off a cougar under any conditions? Further, of the hundreds of spectators watching Flight 90's survivors struggle to survive, only Lenny Skutnik went from being a bystander to a rescuer.

Discussion Questions

1. As you read this essay did any other acts of courage come to mind? If not, either from real life or fiction, can you think of at least one heroic story?
2. It has been said: *Heroes are not born, they are cornered.* What does this maxim imply about courageous behavior?
3. Do you believe that fear must be overcome for an act to be considered courageous?

Suggested Follow-Up

Show the scene from the movie *Courage Under Fire* in which a helicopter pilot faces down the mutiny of her crew.[9] The officer, played by Meg Ryan, provides excellent examples of leadership and courage. The setting for this drama is the Persian Gulf War and the ten-minute climactic scene begins approximately twenty minutes from the movie's end. Also in the movie are Denzel Washington, Matt Damon, and Lou Diamond Phillips.

Chapter VI

Empathy

MY NAME IS JANE DOE TOO! (ANONYMOUS)

Pain is a mechanism for growth. It carves out the heart to make room for compassion.

–Betty Sue Flowers

In the March 9, 1999 Woman's Day *"Back Talk" section appeared an essay written by Paula Spencer. Entitled, "Meet Jane Doe," the author sarcastically wrote about her "dull" and "normal" life—unaffected by depression, addiction, sexual abuse, eating disorders, or any other misfortune. Deriding women who have resorted to psychotherapy, medications, or support groups to deal with such issues as incest, unfaithful spouses, and disabled children, she sardonically confesses to living a normal life. She concluded that she is, "a wholesome plain Jane," and "perfectly proud to be just plain normal."*

Provoked by her lack of empathy, one woman eloquently responded to Paula Spencer's essay. Entitled, "My Name Is Jane Doe Too!" the response was never published by Woman's Day.

I had the opportunity to read "Meet Jane Doe" (a.k.a. Paula Spencer) in your March 9, 1999 BACK TALK article. What I thought was going to be a tongue-in-cheek look at her life, soon proved to cross over the boundaries of compassion, into a judgmental and insensitive view of the real world.

You see my name is Jane Doe too. I grew up in the suburbs, excelled in school, was very active in church, was accepted to a top-notch university, and had all the outer appearances of a "normal" life. I am also an incest survivor—a fact that has affected but not defined me. The abuse was not my fault, I could not have prevented it, and there were no people for me to turn to for help as a teen. I married a man who seemed charming and successful. We were the "perfect couple" in many people's eyes. But, behind closed doors, a dark side of him emerged. After fifteen years of trying to make my marriage work, I am now a single mom. I never wanted or planned this. I spend my time working to make financial ends meet, but more important teaching my children values of respect, perseverance, and courage. The pain they have experienced greatly distresses me, but they know that life is not always easy, is often painful, and can be unpredictable. They are compassionate and sensitive children, who can and will face the challenges of life equipped with a set of skills that only experience brings. I am sorry that Paula (and therefore most likely her children), have no idea of what I am talking about.

You see, I also know many other Jane Does. My friend with a child dying from a genetic degenerative disorder, watches her little girl slip away with time, and must tend to her needs 24 hours a day. She is Jane Doe too. Another Jane Doe I know has cancer, faces a year of chemotherapy and an uncertain prognosis. Then there is the Jane Doe whose husband up and left her for another woman. The list goes on and on.

I work in a rehabilitation hospital, and I have seen hundreds of people's lives changed in an instant by disease, accident, or illness. Paula seems strikingly unaware of the amount of suffering and pain that is a part of everyday life. Do you have blinders on, Paula, or do you simply see these things as reflections of a faulty and weak character?

I am sorry you view your life as dull. Maybe you could fill some of your "normal time" with those who are in need (usually by no fault of their own). Why not try volunteering in a battered woman's shelter, working in a soup kitchen, providing respite care for exhausted families of chronically ill children? Could you volunteer in a hospice, hold the hand of someone vomiting after chemotherapy, or be a consistent and patient friend to someone suffering with depression? Would you dare to give a weary mom a break each week watching her child with ADD?

In the mean time, instead of mocking the suffering of others, please realize you are not immune to what life can hand out. Any day, you or a member of your family could be diagnosed with cancer, killed by a drunk driver, or be the victim of violent crime. If such challenges were to enter your life, I certainly hope you would consider joining a support group, accept counseling, and be willing to alter your over-rated and self-righteous point of view about what is truly "normal."

I would suggest you humbly get on your knees and give thanks to God for the blessings you have experienced. Facing the many common challenges you poked fun at, and doing whatever it takes to rise to those challenges (yes, even if that means taking Prozac or Ritalin), helps one find joy in the small things in life—nothing is taken for granted. I think if you shed some of your self-pride, you will find that your "dull" life will be more fulfilling. And if you truly feel deprived at having no Twelve Step group to go to, may I suggest you have the courage to start your own group—maybe called Pridefulholics Anonymous?

Discussion Questions

1. Empathy is defined as the ability to project one's self in another person's situation and share in another's emotions or feelings. Do you believe that Paula Spencer is "empathically challenged?"
2. Do you believe that the writer of, "My Name Is Jane Doe Too" over-reacted to Paula Spencer's essay and judged her too harshly?

Suggested Follow-Up

Assign students an investigation of Daniel Goleman's *Emotional Intelligence* theory. Have them summarize what emotional intelligence is and why Dr. Goleman believes it is an important characteristic. Direct them to include in their research a description of his thoughts on *empathy*.

Chapter VII

Endurance

THE ICE BOWL

Men wanted for a hazardous journey. Small wages. Bitter cold. Long months of complete darkness. Constant danger. Safe return doubtful. Honour and recognition in case of success!

                     –Ernest Shackleton

In 1914, twenty-seven men responded to Ernest Shackleton's advertisement for crewmen to join an expedition that would be the first to cross Antarctica. Shackleton's foreboding advertisement proved to be understated. Their ship sunk and they endured unspeakable pain as castaways in one of the world's most hostile and frigid environments.

On December 31, 1967 the Green Bay Packers and Dallas Cowboys played for the National Football League championship in a game that came to be known as the Ice Bowl. To equate a football game with the Shackleton expedition would be absurd. Nevertheless, there is value in learning about the greatest display of endurance ever shown on a football field.

"It was as cold as I'll ever be in my life; I'll never be that cold again."[1] With these words Dallas Cowboys safety Mel Renfro spoke for players, coaches, referees, and forty-thousand spectators who endured three hours in Lambeau for a football game played in minus fourteen degree weather with a wind chill factor of minus forty-six. By the game's end, the wind chill had dipped to sixty-nine below zero.

We admire the determination to continue at a task through pain and fatigue. At one time or another we all have experienced the pain of cold. The philosopher René Descartes explained pain as injured nerves sending impulses to the brain—analogous to pulling a rope to ring a bell. However, "Pain is a property not only of the senses of the region where we feel it—but of the brain as well."[2] In fact, the brain can create pain without injured nerves. In phantom limb pain there is no rope to be pulled. Also, the brain records experiences as painful, making it unnecessary to recreate the sensation of pain. Fortunately, we do not have to re-experience the pain of being burned in order to be careful around fire. It is the memory of that painful day that enabled Dallas fullback Don Perkins to say, "Wow, that was one cold mother."[3]

Listening to the stories of those who were there provide us with an appreciation of how cold it was. Television commentator Frank Gifford was incredulous when his 6:00 a.m. hotel wake-up greeted him with, "Good morning Mr. Gifford, the temperature is minus twenty-nine degrees—the coldest New Year's Eve in Green Bay history."[4] Later that day, in the unheated press box, Gifford put a cup of coffee to his lips, realized the coffee had frozen, and said, "It looks like I'm going to have a bite of coffee."[5]

There are two other Ice Bowl stories involving lips. The halftime show was cancelled when the lip of a musician became stuck to his instrument when he began to play. Similarly, on the first play of the game, when a referee pulled his whistle from his mouth, his lip began bleeding. "It bled only for a moment," recalled Cowboys' tackle Bob Lilly, "and then the blood froze almost immediately on his chin."[6]

Under normal conditions the body heat generated by playing a game is sufficient to keep players warm. But the Ice Bowl was not played under normal conditions. Green Bay guard Jerry Kramer, one of the game's heroes, recalled it as the only time he did not eventually warm up from playing. Like the weather, he got colder and colder as the afternoon progressed.

All of the players' efforts to get warm met with failure. Dallas receiver Lance Rentzel recounted that some of his teammates wrapped their feet in saran wrap after hearing that cellophane would resist the cold by retaining heat. Renfro remembered the butane heaters on the sidelines that the players huddled around when they came off the field. The smell of burning rubber alerted several of them that their shoe was too close to the heater and melting. Numb feet made them unaware of a self-inflicted hot-foot.

Cold feet were not the only problem. Packers' linebacker Dave Robinson concealed his disobedience to Coach Vince Lombardi, who insisted that his players not wear gloves. A black man, Robinson wore brown gloves that day. Cold hands neutralized the Cowboy's most dangerous and exciting player, Bob Hayes. Nicknamed "Bullet Bob," Hayes had won the gold medal in the one-hundred-meter dash in the 1964 Olympics. Early in the game the Green Bay defense noted that Hayes tucked his hands in the waistband of his pants if he was being used as a decoy. When a passing play included him as a receiver, he lined up with his hands on his hips. On that day the world's fastest human was the world's coldest wide receiver.

Faces were also a concern. Late in the game Dallas quarterback Don Meredith was unintelligible to his teammates when he tried to call a play in the huddle. It was only after one of them quickly massaged Meredith's frozen face that he could be understood.

The playing field was frozen, making it more like an ice-skating rink than a football field. Packers' fullback Chuck Mercein described getting tackled, "like falling on jagged concrete."[7] Renfro remembered it as, "Jagged ice...that was like taking a razor to your jersey."[8] Rentzel spoke of the eeriness of being on the field and hearing thousands of spectators who could not be seen because of their vaporized breath. "There was this incredible haze of breath," wrote journalist David Maraniss, "Tens of thousands of puffs coming out. Like seeing big buffaloes in an enormous herd on the winter plains. It was prehistoric."[9] Rentzel said it was surreal.

The Green Bay Packers scored the winning touchdown with sixteen seconds remaining in the game. Their 21-17 victory made them no more admirable than the team they defeated. Packer offensive tackle Forrest Gregg estimated, "It's impossible to ask more of a group of players than was asked of them that day."[10] Endurance is the ability to stand up under pain, distress, or fatigue.

Epilogue

Endurance was the name of Ernest Shackleton's ship. It is also the word that accurately describes the players and spectators who braved the bone-rattling cold that made this game the Ice Bowl.

Discussion Questions

1. Only passing consideration was given to postponing the game. Do you think this game should not have been played? Why do you think this game was played in spite of the weather?
2. The author of this essay wrote, "To equate a football game with the Shackleton expedition would be absurd." Do you agree that it is absurd to equate the Ice Bowl with the Antarctic Expedition? If so, why?
3. Read again Ernest Shackleton's advertisement for crewmen. Consider that twenty-seven men responded and went on the expedition. Also consider that not a single Green Bay Packer or Dallas Cowboy refused to play in the Ice Bowl. How do you explain these two instances of the willingness of human beings to endure extreme cold weather?
4. Can you think of similar illustrations of endurance?
5. Under what conditions would you consider endurance a demonstration of foolishness?

Suggested Follow-Up

1. "It was as cold as I'll ever be in my life. I'll never be that cold again," said Dallas Cowboys' safety Mel Renfro. Assign as essay in which students describe the coldest they have ever been.
2. Assign research on Ernest Shackleton's Antarctic expedition, giving specific attention to why people engage in life-threatening expeditions.
3. View the video presentation of the Ice Bowl. It is available as part of The NFL Greatest Games Series.[11]

Chapter VIII

Forgiveness

THE SUNFLOWER

Forgive us our debts, as we also have forgiven our debtors.
                                        –Jesus Christ (Matthew 6:12)

*Forgiveness is the act of relinquishing or avoiding negative
attitudes toward someone for a wrong they have committed.
Distinct from the outward act of telling others they are
forgiven , forgiveness is an inner act or activity; it is a
change of heart from ill will (hatred, anger, or contempt)
to good will. It need not imply a complete reacceptance of a
person, nor a return to the same good relationship we had
with someone. It does, however, open the door to a renewal or
restoration of relationships.*[1]
                                        –Mike W. Martin

*In this essay the act and attitude of forgiveness are considered. What
does it mean to forgive someone? Why is forgiveness a virtue? Does forgiving someone provide a benefit for the one who forgives? These are
the questions addressed in this reflection on forgiveness.*

Holocaust survivor Simon Wiesenthal began his memoir, *The Sun-
flower*, with the description of the day he was escorted to the hospital
room of a dying German soldier who had requested to speak with a
Jew. The soldier was so heavily bandaged that he had a mummy-like

appearance. The nurse informed the soldier that she had brought him a Jew and left the room.

At first, puzzled and afraid, Wiesenthal listened as the man in the bed recounted a horrifying story in which he participated in the killing of a number of Jews by boarding them up in a building and setting it on fire. The soldier went on to explain that recently his body had been blown apart in an explosion and he would soon be dead - within a day or two. Waiting to die, the soldier was being tormented by the screams of the Jewish men, women, and children he had burned alive. He thought if Wiesenthal, a Jew, would forgive him, the screaming would stop and he could die in peace.

In Sherwin Nuland's bestseller, *How We Die*, he begins the grisly account of nine-year-old Katie Mason's murder with these words:

> The entire grim sequence of events—hemorrhage,
> exanguination, cardiac arrest, the agonal moments,
> clinical death, and finally irretrievable mortality –
> was played out during a particularly vicious murder
> committed a few years ago in a small Connecticut city
> not far from the hospital where I work. The attack took
> place at a crowded street fair, in full view of scores of
> people who had fled the scene in fear of the killer's
> maniacal rage. He had never laid eyes on his victim
> before the savage onslaught. She was a buoyant,
> beautiful child of nine.[2]

The man who murdered Katie was a paranoid schizophrenic named Peter Carlquist. He had a long history of violent assaults. "As early as six he had told a psychiatrist that the devil had come up out of the ground and entered his body. Perhaps he was right."[3] Shortly before his attack on Katie an advisory board at the nearby state mental hospital determined that Carlquist could be trusted to sign himself out for several hours at a time. Is it reasonable to imagine Joan Mason, Katie's mother, forgiving Peter Carlquist or the advisory board members who turned him loose to plunge a hunting knife repeatedly into her daughter?

What Is Forgiveness?

Forgiveness is a state of mind expressed by inaction. The state of mind is the result of the hard choice to neither resent someone nor desire misfortune for that person. The inaction is not pursuing punishment for an offense or payment for a debt. Moreover, forgiveness is not forgetting. If we could will to forget an injurious act it would be unnecessary to forgive. Forgiveness does not result in a clean slate such that an individual's prior behavior has no influence on future interactions. Jesus Christ, who taught recurringly on forgiveness, also instructed on the importance of "counting the cost" when making decisions.[4]

Why Is Forgiveness a Virtue?

Forgiveness meets Aristotle's characterization of a virtue as the mean between two vices. Forgiveness is not as extreme as vengeance; neither is it as extreme as denial—pretending that an offense has not occurred. People obsessed with getting even cannot forget; those in denial make believe they cannot remember. Forgiveness requires remembering without desiring revenge.

Plato considered a behavior virtuous if it conformed to an individual's spirit. He believed that the human mind consisted of three main parts: reason, appetites, and spirit. Reason's function is to control the body and maintain honorable conduct. The appetites direct the satisfaction of physical cravings, some of which are undesirable urges. The spirited element, which can be understood as a sense of pride, supports reason in controlling the appetites. When people who consider forgiveness a virtue practice it they are conforming their behavior to their spirited element. When people live up to standards of virtue they have set for themselves they are conducting themselves honorably.

Also, forgiveness is a virtue because it requires self-discipline. Self-discipline is the ability to do what ought to be done regardless of feelings. Forgiving is an act of self-discipline when a person can say, "My feelings are screaming, 'Revenge!'" but I choose to forgive because of the kind of person I want to be."

Does Forgiveness Provide a Benefit for the One Who Forgives?

There are at least three advantages for people who choose to forgive. First, the act of conforming their behavior to their predetermined standard contributes to character development. C.S. Lewis said that with each of life's moral decisions we make ourselves a little more a creature of heaven or a little more a creature of hell.

Second, the exercise of self-discipline contributes to adulthood. Sigmund Freud characterized an adult (ego) as someone who consistently controls the impulse for immediate gratification (id). Each decision to forgive, if acted upon, makes a person more of an adult and less of a child.

Third, when a choice is made to act according to a philosophical or religious ideal it is a demonstration of submission. In his moral stages theory, psychologist Lawrence Kohlberg described the highest level of moral reasoning as adherence to basic ethical principles. The choice to submit to a moral code recognized as commendable is characteristic of people who are neither living whimsically nor governed by impulses.

Conclusion

Philosopher Dennis Prager has written, "forgiveness is contingent on the sinner repenting and it can be given only by the one sinned against."[5] Simon Wiesenthal did not forgive the dying German soldier who asked to be forgiven. Wiesenthal reasoned that he could not forgive on behalf of others. Forgiveness is a real-life issue for everyone. Throughout life people are challenged to request it for themselves and extend it to others.

Discussion Questions

1. From literature, movies or real life, are you familiar with any noteworthy acts of forgiveness?
2. Do you agree with the author's position that forgiveness is a virtue and beneficial for the one who forgives?
3. Do you agree with Simon Wiesenthal's decision to not forgive the soldier?
4. One of the statements made by Jesus when being crucified was, "Father, forgive them, for they do not know what they are doing."[6] In his situation, for whom do you believe Jesus was asking forgiveness? Do you believe the mentally ill man who killed Katie Mason should be forgiven because he did not know what he was doing?

Suggested Follow-Up

The lawyer and author John Grisham wrote *A Time to Kill*, a story based on the actual trial of a father who killed two men who savagely raped and beat his daughter. Either assign this book or view its movie version.[7] The cast includes Sandra Bullock, Samuel L. Jackson, Matthew McConaughy, Kevin Spacey, and Donald and Kiefer Sutherland.

Chapter IX

Happiness

WHO IS HAPPY AND WHY?

How to gain, how to keep, how to recover happiness is in fact for most men at all times the secret motive for all they do.

–William James

Motivation is the drive or need that energizes and directs behavior. It explains why we do what we do. It is not an overstatement to say that all of psychology is the study of motivation. For psychologists, happiness is not an uninterrupted state of feeling good and well-being. For them it is a self-perceived satisfaction with life - an overall contentment with the conditions of one's life.

Twenty-three centuries ago Aristotle defined happiness as, "an activity of the soul in accord with highest virtue."[1] In the following essay the compatibility between Aristotle's definition and the findings of psychological research are striking.

Respond to each of the following statements with an evaluation of true or false. When considering these statements, think of happiness as a *self-perceived satisfaction with life - an overall contentment with the conditions of one's life.*

1. Wealthy people are happier than people with average incomes.
2. People who are physically challenged (e.g. blindness, paralysis, or amputation) are less happy than people who are not physically challenged.
3. Elderly people are less happy than middle-aged and young people.
4. People who have a religious faith are happier than people who do not have a religious faith.
5. People are happier at work than at leisure.
6. Married people are happier than unmarried people.
7. People living in democracies are happier than people living in dictatorial or totalitarian states.
8. People who have won millions of dollars in a lottery are very happy compared to most people.
9. Some people are born happy and remain that way throughout their lifetime.
10. People can be happy by making up their mind to be happy.

For the correctness of these statements according to research look under **Discussion Questions** at the end of this essay. (You might want to do this before reading further since the essay provides information that will give the correct response to most of the statements.)

Everything for which people strive is intermediate to the ultimate goal of happiness. "If I could just find that right person then I'd be happy." "I'll be happy when I finish school." "When I land the right job I'll be happy." "I won't be happy until these bills are paid off." "I need to lick this cancer and be healthy again, then I'll be happy." Nobody ever says "I want to be happy so that…" Happiness is the ultimate goal. Happiness is invariably what parents most want for their children: "I don't care if they're rich, I just want them to be happy."

Implicit in all of these statements is the recognition that happiness is not a continuous state of elevated mood but an overall contentedness with life. Only addicts seek a life of uninterrupted euphoria. Psychiatrist Scott Peck characterized addiction as the sacred disease because of addicts' determination to live a paradisical life in which pain is never experienced. Except for addicts, everyone seems to recognize that elevated moods are transitory. Bars offer a Friday happy hour, implicitly admitting that one hour is the best alcohol has to offer. Photo albums are maintained to document rare and fleeting special occasions of happiness. Literally, living "happily ever after" is a fairytale existence. Psychologists are not alone in their recognition that if happiness is to have a connection with reality it must be defined as an overall contentment with life.

Psychologists have not disregarded the human need or desire to achieve happiness. Erik Erikson's eight-stage psychosocial theory of development theorizes that in old age people reflect on life, asking the question: *Am I content with how I have lived my life?* In recent years psychological research has been more attentive to positive psychology - the life conditions that correlate with life satisfaction - than in previous years.

This research has produced findings that have established four life conditions that correlate with happiness. (A correlation is not a cause-and-effect relationship. A correlation exists when two conditions tend to occur together calling for further investigation. Cause and effect relationships are rare. They exist when event - A precedes event - B and it is the irrefutable, demonstrable conclusion that event - A is the cause of event - B.)

What are the life conditions that correlate with happiness? While there might be more than four, there are at least that many according to psychological investigation.

1. Happiness and Activity

For more than two decades Mihalyi Csikszentmihalyi studied *flow* - the optimal experiences during which people reported feelings of engrossment and enjoyment. He discovered that flow experiences are characterized by an absence of a sense of time and a loss of self-awareness. Csikszentmihalyi found that it is true that time flies by when you're having a good time. He wrote, "One of the most common descriptions of optimal experience is that time no longer seems to pass the way it ordinarily does."[2]

Concerning the loss of self-awareness, consider how unpleasant it is to be self-conscious - to feel awkward or embarrassed as an object of notice. There is no self-consciousness during flow. Csikszentmihalyi also concluded that happiness is like sawdust. Just as sawdust is the by-product of the activity of sawing wood, the experience of happiness occurs as a by-product of engagement in some activity. Often, so much attention is given to the activity that happiness is realized only in retrospect.

It is ironic that people who consciously pursue happiness are least likely to attain it. Scott Peck observed that the conscious determination to be happy prevents addicts and narcissists from achieving contentedness. The addict's effort to live a life of uninterrupted bliss results in a life mismanaged and, paradoxically, unhappiness.

Similar to the addict's fate is that of the narcissist. Preoccupied with the self to the point of self-absorption, the narcissist goes through life oblivious to opportunities for enjoyment and happiness. Milo Ray Phelps' poem has captured the self-defeating plight of the narcissist.

> Elizabeth Bates has been to Rome
> And looked at the statues there;
> Elizabeth Bates has scaled the Alps
> And sniffed at the mountain air.
> Elizabeth Bates has winced at Nice
> And quibbled at gay Paree,
> And lifted her delicate eyebrows at
> Indelicate barbary.
> Elizabeth Bates has "done" the globe
> From Panama back to the states,
> But all she saw on the way around
> Was Miss Elizabeth Bates.
> Elizabeth Bates has been to Spain
> And sampled her ego there,
> And viewed the face of a thoughtful sphinx
> And paused to arrange her hair.
> Elizabeth Bates can be no place
> She hasn't been there before,
> But has never yet been out of herself,
> So I have traveled more![3]

Researchers on happiness seem to have reached the same conclusion as Aristotle: that engagement in some activity correlates with happiness.

2. Happiness and Satisfaction with What One Has

In *Happiness Is a Serious Problem* philosopher Dennis Prager wrote of "the missing tile syndrome," in which he told the story of being in a beautifully tiled bathroom that had one tile missing.[4] When he realized that his eyes were drawn to the room's single flaw, it occurred to him that it was a metaphor for how unhappy people look at life. Giving disproportionate attention to something that is missing and allowing it to obscure what is present and available to be enjoyed is a characteristic of discontented people. Prager's story brings to mind Abraham Lincoln's observation that most people are about as happy as they make up their minds to be.

Perhaps it is focusing on what one does not have that explains why a study has shown that lottery winners are no happier than the population at large. If this is true it gives credibility to Oscar Wilde's assessment that, "There are only two tragedies in life. Not getting what you want and getting what you want."[5]

3. Happiness and Self-Satisfaction

There is a story about Sir Winston Churchill at a formal dinner party. Finding himself in the company of snobbish, pretentious guests, the hostess approached him and asked, "Mr. Churchill, are you enjoying yourself?"

"Yes," he replied, "and that is about all."

To be satisfied with one's self is neither arrogant nor narcissistic. Recall that Aristotle said that overall contentment in life requires living, "in accord with highest virtue." Aristotle believed that people cannot be happy living in violation of their moral code. Self-satisfaction requires a life of consistency with one's stated values.

In what is perhaps the most famous teaching ever given, the Sermon on the Mount, Jesus Christ taught on happiness by instructing how people ought to live so that they could live with themselves.

4. Happiness and Living in the Present

It has been said that life is a present to be lived in the present. Psychiatrist W. Beran Wolfe expressed this sentiment with these words: "One important source of unhappiness is the habit of putting off living to some fictional future date."[6] Living in the present does not mean living only in the moment and always seeking immediate gratification. It does not require a great imagination to envision the disastrous consequences of a life driven by impulse. Instead it means not being described by the poem, "Mr. Meant To."

Mr. Meant To has a comrade,
And his name is Didn't Do;
Have you ever chanced to meet them?
Did they ever call on you?
These two fellows live together
In the house of never win,
And I'm told that it is haunted
By the ghost of Might-Have Been.[7]

Conclusion

It has been said that any man who believes at forty what he believed at twenty hasn't been paying attention. In his biography, boxing legend Muhammed Ali reflected on his pursuit of happiness as a young man.

I used to chase women all the time. And I won't say
it was right, but look at all the temptations I had. I was
young, handsome, heavyweight champion of the world.
Women were always offering themselves to me. I had
two children by women I wasn't married to. I love them;
they're my children. I feel just as good and proud of them
as I do my other children, but that wasn't the right thing
to do. And running around, living that kind of life, wasn't
good for me. It hurt my wife, it offended God. It never
really made me happy. But ask any man who's forty
years old—if he knew at twenty what he knows now,
would he do things different? Most people would. So
I did wrong; I'm sorry. And all I'll say as far as running
around chasing women is concerned, is that's all past. I've
got a good wife now, and I'm lucky to have her.[8]

Discussion Questions

For discussion review the ten questions given at the start of the essay. When considering the answers given below note the cited research supporting each answer.

Answers

1. False: Ed Diener and Robert Biswas-Diener, "Will money increase subjective well-being?" *Social Indicators Research,* February 2002.

2. False: David Myers. *The Pursuit of Happiness: Who Is Happy and Why.* New York: William Morrow and Company, Inc., 1992.
3. False: Martin Pinquat, et al. "Age differences in perceived positive affect balance in middle and old age," *Journal of Happiness Studies, 2001.*
4. True: David Myers.
5. True: Mihalyi Csikszentmihalyi. *Flow: The Psychology of Optimal Experience.* New York: Harper-Collins. 1990.
6. True: David Myers.
7. True: Ronald Inglehart and Hans-Dieter Klingemann, "Genes, culture democracy, and happiness," in Ed Diener and Eunkook Suh (Editors), *Culture and Subjective Well-Being,* MIT Press, 2000.
8. False: Unfulfilled Lottery Winners: ABC New Special Report, "The Mystery of Happiness," January 22, 1998. (See www.abcnews .com/2020/.
9. True: Thomas J. Bouchard, Jr. et al. "Sources of Human Psychological Differences: The Minnesota Study of Twins Reared Apart, Science, October 1990.
10. True: Interview with Dr. David Meyers, author of *The Pursuit of Happiness: Who Is Happy and Why.* This part of the interview is in John Stossel's *Myths, Lies, and Downright Stupidity.* (New York: Hyperion, 2006), p. 278.

Suggested Follow-Up

The television program "20/20" presented a special report that is available on video. It is a forty-five minute presentation entitled: "The Mystery of Happiness," January 22, 1998. Its cost is approximately fifty dollars and can be acquired by contacting www.abcnews.com/2020.[9]

Chapter X

Honesty

THE PASTOR AND THE PIE

A dilemma is a situation in which no matter what you choose you are wrong.

—Oscar Wilde

As children, we are taught to tell the truth. As we experience more of life we are likely to encounter situations that provoke the question: Is it ever morally right to tell a lie? A dilemma is a situation in which a choice must be made between two unpleasant alternatives. In the following true story, a pastor finds himself in a dilemma.

The pastor always moved to the back of the sanctuary when the congregation was singing the closing hymn. From there he would give the benediction and dismiss his flock. He would then place himself just inside the front door so that he could individually greet the congregants as they exited the church. The pastor enjoyed this concluding ritual and his parishioners never seemed to mind the five or so minutes it required.

An elderly widow was one of the last to receive the pastor's wish for a "good Sabbath." She was the kind of woman to be found in every church, regardless of denomination, and deferentially referred to as "Sister". The pastor was unable to cup her frail and withered hand gently in both of his because she was carrying a pie. Reminiscent of a child presenting a straight-A report card to a parent, Sister could barely contain her excitement as she gave it to him. Regaining the breath she had spent transporting the pie, Sister managed, "Pastor, I hope you and your family enjoy this pie."

The pastor knew that for this woman, baking a pie was a herculean labor. He responded, "Thank you so much. This will be our dessert today. Have a blessed Sabbath, Sister."

That afternoon, after dinner, the pie's tin foil covering was removed. This unveiling released a delightful aroma that was immediately recognized as rhubarb. A slice was cut for each member of the family while the pastor informed them their dessert was a gift from Sister. As they had been taught, the children waited until everyone at the table had been served before eating. With the coordination of a team of synchronized swimmers, they placed the first forkful of pie into their mouths. Too refined to spit out the unpalatable morsels, the pastor and his family swallowed their first—and last—taste of Sister's pie.

Stunned silence was followed by parents and children looking each to the other for unspoken confirmation that in a world with millions of pies they had just sampled the most uneatable. The phrase, "It goes without saying" was made for a moment like this. There was no need for anyone to comment on the pie's odious quality and its assault upon their sense of taste. The pastor's wife broke the silence, "What are you going to tell Sister?"

Of course, the question was rhetorical as well as unnecessary. The wastebasket was circulated to receive each uneaten piece of the pie followed by the half that remained in the pie tin.

That week the pastor spent as much time contemplating the answer to his wife's question as he spent preparing his sermon. She asked the question as a clear declaration of the dilemma awaiting her husband the next Sunday. What is one to do with the truth when it would hurt someone, serving no good purpose? To tell Sister that her pie was delicious would compromise the truth, sparing her feelings. However, it might encourage her to inflict another pie on his family with other pies to follow. He felt the full weight of simultaneous obligations to the truth and the protection of Sister's feelings. The pastor also wrestled with the concurrent and conflicting duties to speak truthfully as a good example for his children and protect them from another one of Sister's pies.

The next Sunday morning, the pastor's thoughts alternated between his sermon and the impending encounter with Sister. He had no idea what he was going to say to her. He needed Solomon's wisdom and identified with the king when he was confronted with two women claiming the same baby. "Perhaps, like Solomon," thought the pastor, "what I should say will come to me when I need to say it."

The sermon was delivered, closing hymn sung, and benediction given. The congregants, including Sister, formed the queue for the pastoral greeting. Sister, unencumbered by a pie this time, extended her hand. Before he could say, "Good Sabbath," she asked the question:

"Pastor, did you and your family enjoy the rhubarb pie?"

With neither rehearsal nor hesitation he responded, "Let me tell you something Sister, a pie like that doesn't last long around our house!"

Discussion Questions

1. Did the Pastor lie to Sister when he said, "A pie like that doesn't last long around our house"?
2. Is it ever ethical to tell a lie? If so, under what conditions would lying be morally right? What is one to do with the truth when it would hurt someone and serve no good purpose?
3. Have you ever had to wrestle with a dilemma similar to the one that confronted the pastor?

Suggested Follow-Up

In the Hebrew Bible (Old Testament) in the historical book 1 Kings, Chapter 3, verses 16-28 is a narrative recounting the decision of King Solomon referred to in this story. After reading this narrative, discuss whether or not it is an example of a dilemma. Also discuss if it is an example of wisdom.

Chapter XI

Humility

ELIE WIESEL: AN EXCEPTIONAL TEACHER

One looks back with appreciation to the brilliant teachers, but with gratitude to those who touched our human feelings.

–Carl Jung, Psychiatrist

What are the characteristics of an exceptionally effective teacher? One way of approaching this question is to consider the best teachers you've ever had. This question was asked of 361 Le Moyne College students in a study conducted from 1996 to 2005.[1] In this research the students provided descriptions of the teachers which included specific behaviors and personality traits. After completing this research I wrote a tribute to an exceptionally effective teacher I experienced at Boston University: Professor Elie Wiesel, Holocaust survivor and 1986 Nobel Prize laureate.

Recently I accomplished research in which 361 Le Moyne College students provided information concerning exceptionally effective teachers. In this study the students selected and described a teacher who they have experienced as outstanding. Their descriptions included specific behaviors and characteristics they believe account for these teachers' exceptional effectiveness. While examining and organizing the data, it occurred to me that I, too, have benefited from an extraordinary teacher. His name is Elie Wiesel.

As a doctoral student at Boston University, in the fall of 1987 I was fortunate to have found a place in Professor Wiesel's course: *Literature of Memory: Responses to Jewish Persecution.* In this course we studied literary works describing the kinds of persecution the Jewish people have undergone and the responses of the Christian, Islamic, and Jewish communities to these afflictions. In eighteen years of teaching since then, I have come to recognize Professor Wiesel's favorable influence on my work. As a result of my research on effective teaching, I am able to be more specific in describing his influence. It is not accidental that this essay reads like a tribute to my former teacher. It is my intention to honor him.

The ten characteristics of exceptional teachers most often cited in my investigation are:

1. challenging with reasonable, high expectations—23%
2. sense of humor—16%
3. enthusiastic—15%
4. caring—11%
5. explains complicated material well—11%
6. available to students—8%
7. interested in students—8%
8. made material relevant—5%
9. humble—3%
10. patient listener—3%

As a teacher, Elie Wiesel demonstrated all of these qualities and I could provide anecdotes that would illustrate how he did so. Instead, I have decided to share several memories from the class that have made me want to be a better teacher and person.

If a student raised a hand while Professor Wiesel was lecturing, he would stop speaking to respond immediately to the student's question or comment. A careful listener, he considered teaching an act of service. As the provider of a service, he believed a student's question or comment merited attention without delay.

In 1986 he was awarded the Nobel Peace Prize. Although he had attained international recognition as a prolific author and spokesman for peace, none of his books were on the required reading list for the course. Further, I cannot recall a single time in class when he referred to anything he had written. I remember Elie Wiesel as a man of uncommon humility.

His course is the only one I ever had that included the requirement of a one-hour, individual meeting with the professor. One of the teaching assistants explained this requirement: "Professor Wiesel believes it is important to know his students." We were instructed that in our time with him we could ask him any questions. Also, we were told that he would be asking questions in order to become more familiar with us. In my hour with him I perceived a genuine curiosity and interest in the parts of my life that I shared with him.

Each class meeting Professor Wiesel entered the room from the rear and proceeded to his place in the front. He would acknowledge the students who greeted him along the way by coming to a full stop, making eye contact, recognizing the student by name, and returning the greeting. More from him than anyone else, I learned the importance and value of respecting students.

In an essay entitled *The Disparity Between Intellect and Character* John Robert Coles tells the moving story of an academically capable student who decided to transfer from Harvard because she experienced it as an unfriendly place.[2] It was her observation that faculty, staff, and students interacted with each other in an uncaring, unkind manner. Dr. Coles concludes his essay with a challenge to the academic community, calling for excellence in civility as well as scholarship. Elie Wiesel has met this challenge.

In a tribute to his father, the late Leonard Buscaglia describes a family ritual on which his father insisted. At dinner time each of his children was required to share at least one new thing he or she had learned that day. A professor of education, Leonard Buscaglia reflected on this ritual from his childhood with these words:

> In retrospect, after years of studying how people learn, I realize what a dynamic educational technique Papa was offering us, reinforcing the value of continual learning. Without being aware of it, our family was growing together, sharing experiences, and participating in one another's education. Papa was, without knowing it, giving us an education in the most real sense.
>
> By looking at us, listening to us, hearing us, respecting our opinions, affirming our value, giving us a sense of dignity, he was unquestionably our most influential teacher.[3]

Buscaglia's words also provide an apt description of Elie Wiesel, my exceptionally effective teacher.

Discussion Questions

1. Are you familiar with any of Elie Wiesel's books? (His best known book is *Night*, first published in 1958 and a bestseller as recently as 2006.) If you are familiar with any of his writings, did this description of him as a teacher surprise you?
2. What are your thoughts concerning the ten characteristics of exceptionally effective teachers presented in this essay? Who are some exceptional teachers you've experienced? What behaviors and/or characteristics made them exceptional to you?

Suggested Follow-Up

In the movie *Dead Poets Society* Robin Williams plays Mr. Keating, a dynamic and ingenious English teacher at an exclusive private school. Two scenes, both approximately five minutes in length, are guaranteed to generate discussion of the characteristics of an exceptionally effective teacher. The first scene is the *carpe diem* scene in which Mr. Keating takes his class to the foyer to look at pictures in the school's trophy case and consider the brevity of life. The second scene, starting approximately ten minutes after the end of the *carpe diem* scene, shows Mr. Keating insisting that his students rip the introductory pages out of their textbooks.[4]

Chapter XII

Integrity

FRANCESCA'S DECISION

Our friends are less than perfect. We accept their imperfections and pride ourselves on our sense of reality. But when it comes to love we stubbornly cling to our illusions—to conscious and unconscious visions of how things should be. When it comes to love—to romantic love and sexual love and married love—we have to learn again, with difficulty, how to let go of all kinds of expectations...We sometimes may hate the married state for domesticating our dreams of romantic love.

–Judith Viorst

In 1992 a literary phenomenon appeared: Robert James Waller's The Bridges of Madison County. *After a run of almost 150 weeks on the* New York Times *bestseller list (thirty-eight weeks as number one), it surpassed* Gone With the Wind *as the best-selling hardcover fiction book of all time.*

Not surprising is that the reviews of Waller's romance novel comprise a spectrum.. Critics' evaluations range from "sappy" to "superb." However, even those who consider the story of Robert Kincaid and Francesca Johnson banal are obliged to account for the book's undeniable popularity. (It has been translated into twenty-five languages and sold over twelve million copies). Perhaps the explanation for this story's worldwide acceptance is Francesca's conflict between desire and duty. Psychiatrist Thomas Szasz has written: "The quality of our life depends

largely on concordance or discordance between our desires and our du-
ties. If we can define and experience our duty as our desire—then we
are happy, well-adjusted, normal."[1] *In this essay the disharmony be-*
tween Francesca's desire and duty is explored.

In the late summer of 1965, Robert Kincaid stopped at an Iowa farm-
house to ask directions. There he encountered Francesca Johnson, alone
at home while her husband and two children were visiting the Illinois
State Fair. Robert, a fifty-two-year-old photographer on assignment for
National Geographic, was seeking the location of seven covered bridges
for a photo shoot. As he approached the middle-aged woman on the front
porch he saw that, "She was lovely, or had been at one time, or could be
again."[2] With this encounter began a four-day romance, "an erotic, bit-
tersweet tale of lingering memories and forsaken possibilities."[3]

Author Robert James Waller makes no attempt through his characters
to justify this adultery. His elegant prose describes and explains their
passion without excusing their behavior. On the eve of the return of
Francesca's husband and children, she refuses Kincaid's offer to leave
with him. With these words she speaks of her lackluster life:

> Yes, it's boring in a way. My life, that is. It lacks romance,
> eroticism, dancing in the kitchen to candlelight, and the
> wonderful feel of a man who knows how to love a woman.
> Most of all, it lacks you. But there's this damn sense of
> responsibility I have. To Richard, to the children. Just my
> leaving, taking away my physical presence, would be
> enough for Richard. That alone might destroy him... As much
> as I want you and want to be with you and part of you, I can't
> tear myself away from the realness of my responsibilities.[4]

She goes on to explain that if she left with him she would take with her
the thoughts of her responsibilities.

"If I did leave now, those thoughts would turn me into something
other than the woman you have come to love."[5]

He understood Francesca's decision. "Robert Kincaid was silent. He
knew what she was saying about the road and responsibilities and how
the guilt could transform her. He knew she was right, in a way."[6]

Waller wrote that Kincaid knew Francesca's decision was right *in a*
way. Does this also imply that *in a way* her decision was wrong? The

study of human morals, character, and conduct is the concern of philosophy. Specifically, ethical philosophy is engaged in the question: What should we do? It is no easy task to determine what the obligations of human beings are. The seventh of the Ten Commandments is, "Thou shalt not commit adultery." Yet, nowhere in *The Bridges of Madison County* is adultery referred to as a sin. Francesca's decision to remain with her family was not the result of a religiously motivated confession and repentance. Instead, she explains her decision in terms of her responsibilities to her husband and children. After weighing desire against duty, the scale tipped in favor of duty and she decided to remain an Iowa farmer's wife. Why did the scale tilt toward duty?

The list of ethical philosophers who have pondered the question of right conduct is impressive. It is a list that includes Thomas Hobbes, Immanuel Kant, Søren Kierkegaard, John Stuart Mill, and Friedrich Nietzsche. Some from this list argued that a behavior is right or wrong according to the results it produces. They would say that Kincaid and Francesca's adultery was not wrong because it did not hurt anybody. Others from the list argued that some behaviors are right and others wrong regardless of the results they produce. These philosophers would say that adultery is morally wrong even if it does not hurt an innocent party because it is a forbidden act. Of course, that raises the question: *What makes an act forbidden?* If the answer is the Ten Commandments, does this mean that even people who have no belief in God have a moral obligation to obey the Decalogue. Further, is belief in God necessary for moral behavior? Do people need God in order to be good? All of this is to say that the assignment of *right* and *wrong* to behavior is a complicated endeavor with a long history in philosophy.

Neither have psychologists ignored moral behavior. The late Lawrence Kohlberg's research produced a theory that represents his answer to the question: *By what process do people determine right behavior?* In summary, Kohlbergy's Moral Stages Theory proposes that a behavior is deemed right according to one of six criteria. A behavior is right if it:

1. prevents punishment
2. results in a reward
3. meets with peers' or social approval
4. conforms to the law or social rules

5. deviates from the law or social rules in order to accomplish a greater good (e.g. It is right to tell a lie in order to save a life?)
6. conforms to a universal imperative (e.g. the Hindu teaching of ahisma; nonviolence to all living things.)[7]

Nowhere in the 171 pages of *The Bridges of Madison County* is adultery addressed as a moral issue. Waller made no effort to condemn Kincaid and Francesca's amour as illicit or condone it as romantic. It is only when Francesca explains to her lover why she will not leave with him that a moral issue is considered. Citing her responsibility to her family, Francesca implies that it would be wrong for her to abandon her husband and children. Further, she offers two practical considerations. The guilt she would experience from such abandonment would outweigh the joy of being with Kincaid. Also, the woman he loves would be no more if she selfishly pursued her happiness at the expense of Richard and her children.

When a person is characterized as having integrity, it means that the individual is morally upstanding and honorable. By committing adultery did Francesca lose her integrity? If so, by choosing to remain with her family, did she regain it?

Discussion Questions

1. The essay concluded with two questions: By committing adultery did Francesca lose her integrity? If so, by choosing to remain with her family, did she regain it?
2. Perhaps you have heard it said, "We have a right to our happiness" If Francesca would have been happy leaving with Robert Kincaid did that give her the right to do so?
3. Psychiatrist Thomas Szasz has written:

> Like the Jews waiting for their Messiah, women wait
> for their man—each for their own "savior." Somewhere,
> deep in their hearts, women expect, hope against hope,
> for happiness with the "right" man, with the man whose
> love will give meaning to their lives.[8]

Do you agree with Dr. Szasz's observation? If so, do you think his assessment also applies to men?

4. The story of Robert and Francesca is used in this book as part of a discussion of integrity. How could this story also have been used as part of a discussion of self-discipline or loyalty?

Suggested Follow Up

1. View the movie version of *The Bridges of Madison County* in which Meryl Streep plays Francesca and Clint Eastwood is cast as Robert Kincaid.[9]
2. Assign and discuss this book. Even a relatively slow and deliberate reader could read it in approximately four hours. The discussion should include a consideration of its remarkable popularity. Even if it is nothing more than a banal romance story, why is it the best-selling hardcover fiction of all time?

JOE LOUIS' DEBT

Joe Louis is a credit to his race, the human race.

–Jimmy Cannon

Integrity is the quality of being of sound moral principle. People with integrity are honest, sincere, and honorable. In 1992, Fred Rogers ("Mister Rogers") addressed integrity when speaking at the Boston University commencement: "Always behave in such a way that you'll never be ashamed of the truth about yourself." Boxing legend Joe Louis never had to be ashamed of the truth about himself. Joe Louis showed himself to be a man of integrity in his toughest fight, the one he had with the Internal Revenue Service.

The concerned doctor carefully studied Joe Louis' swollen and lumpy face.

"Joe, you can't fight for at least three months," said Dr. Vincent Nardiello as he shone his small flashlight into the fighter's eyes.

"Doc," Louis responded, "Do you mind if I don't fight any more at all?"[1]

On the morning of October 26, 1951 Jimmy Cannon described middle-aged, battle-worn Joe Louis:

He is an honorable man of simple dignity who works at
the dirtiest of all games with a crude nobility. As a pugilist
this is a guy whose deportment matches his skills. Even now,
at thirty-seven, slow and often clumsy, Louis is a reliable
performer. The errors he makes are caused by a disobedient
body. But his gameness is unimpaired and his intentions are
pure.[2]

Cannon's sentimentality for the man who was the heavyweight champion of the world for eleven years came from memories like the one in 1948 after the first Joe Wolcott fight. Although Louis won, "His face was swollen. He looked like a loser." Before Cannon could ask his first post-fight interview question, Louis remembered that Cannon had not been feeling well and asked him, "How's your cold?"[3]

On October 26, 1951 Joe Louis stepped into the ring to face Rocky Marciano in a non-title fight. Louis had retired in 1949, leaving the title to be claimed first by Ezzard Charles and then Joe Wolcott. Marciano was a rising star who would eventually wrest the heavyweight championship from Wolcott. Well aware that his best days were behind him, Louis came out of retirement in 1950 intending to earn enough money to settle a $500,000 tax debt owed to the Internal Revenue Service.

Generosity, patriotism, reckless spending, and misplaced trust combined to erode the fortune he had accumulated over a seventeen-year career.

When he earned over $371,000 in his first two years as a
professional boxer, Louis immediately helped family and friends
all over the country. For example, he voluntarily paid back to the
government welfare payments his stepfather had received during
the Great Depression... one month after the bombing of Pearl
Harbor, the generous Louis gave his entire $65,200 fee (about
$700,000 in today's money) from a fight to the Naval Relief
Fund. Less than three months later, he gave his $45,882 purse
from another fight (about $500,000 today) to the Army Relief
Fund. Ever the Patriot, he halted his lucrative boxing career
and enlisted as a private, earning only $21 a month.[4]

Ironically, the total of Louis' donations to the war effort ($111,082) was nearly equal to his original tax debt ($117,000). Unfortunately, by the time the I.R.S. made him aware of his debt the interest on it increased it to over a million dollars. In addition to the original debt he was being taxed on the money he was earning in his effort to pay off the debt. Reflecting on this Sisyphean task, he said "When you owe that kind of money you can't get out...it's like doing roadwork on a treadmill. The faster you run, the faster they move that treadmill against you"[5]

It's unfortunate that of the innumerable photographs of Joe Louis, the one most famous is from the Marciano fight and the least indicative of Louis' greatness. It shows him dazed and flat of his back, his body draped over the ring's bottom rope. Marciano felt so bad about the beating he gave his boyhood idol that Rocky cried and apologized to Louis after the fight. The ex-champion thanked the future champion for agreeing to the match and an opportunity for a payday. Louis earned $135,000 that night, most of which he turned over to the I.R.S.

Regrettable is that the Marciano fight was not the Brown Bomber's final humiliation. Although it was his last boxing match, it was not the last time he entered the ring. Desperate for money, in 1956 he turned to professional wrestling. Balding and paunchy, Louis was as embarrassed by his aging body as by the pseudo-athletic farce in which he was participating. Before his quixotic effort to settle with the I.R.S. was over, he would further lower himself by appearing on television game shows. Even when he and his wife, Rose, managed to win $60,000 on the show *High Finance*, his $30,000 share went to the I.R.S. As if to prove that humiliation knows no depth, the champion traveled with a circus as a make-believe lion tamer. Armed with a whip, he feigned mastery over a lion who, like Louis, had grown old and devitalized.

It has been said that the members of the United States Congress would vote to exempt themselves from the law of gravity if they could. Yet, Congress showed no regard for Louis' wartime generosity when they voted to reject a bill proposed by Alfred Sieminski (Democrat, New Jersey) to forgive Louis' tax debt. Those who voted "no" on that proposal seem quite unlike the man of whom sportswriter Milton Gross wrote: "He was a symbol of integrity. He was a man of unimpeachable pride and steadfast principle."[6]

Discussion Questions

1. Integrity is the quality of being morally upright, honest, and honorable. Do you believe Joe Louis demonstrated integrity or weakness in his effort to pay the tax debt he owed the I.R.S.?

2. When drafted to serve in the United States Army during the Vietnam War, boxing champion Muhammed Ali refused induction into the service as a conscientious objector; one who refuses to participate in warfare as a matter of conviction against killing. Ali was tried and convicted as a draft evader. (The Supreme Court later ruled in his favor on appeal). Does Muhammed Ali's refusal to enter the military make him less a patriot than Joe Louis? In spite of their contrasting responses to the government, is it possible that both men demonstrated integrity?

Suggested Follow-Up

There is an excellent presentation of Joe Louis' life in the context of World War II and his subsequent financial problems in the HBO Home Video *The Kings of the Ring*. The part of the video featuring Louis is approximately fifteen minutes in length. It also includes an approximate fifteen-minute description of Muhammed Ali's career, including his refusal to enter the United States Army. [7]

Chapter XIII

Loyalty

URIAH (II SAMUEL 11:1-27)

I am loyal to a fault. I have many faults and I am loyal to all of them.
                                                                    –Steve Allen

What would make the leader of a nation risk his place in history as well as his marriage by committing adultery and further compromise his integrity with a cover-up? The Hebrew Bible (a.k.a. the Old Testament) unflinchingly recounts the infidelity of its greatest king, David, in the historical book of II Samuel. This narrative includes a description of the loyalty of one of David's soldiers, Uriah, the husband of the woman with whom the king committed adultery.

Psychiatrist Thomas Szasz wrote, "The quality of our life depends largely on concordance or discordance between our desires and our duties."[1] In the story that follows, King David is the picture of unrestrained desire while Uriah is the personification of duty.

In the spring, at the time when kings go off to war, David sent Joab out with the king's men and the whole Israelite army. They destroyed the Ammonites and besieged Rabbah. But David remained in Jerusalem. One evening David got up from his bed and walked around on the roof of the palace. From the roof he saw a woman bathing. The woman was very beautiful, and David sent someone to find out about her. The man said, "Isn't this Bathsheba, the daughter of Eliam and the wife of Uriah the Hittite?" Then David sent messengers to get her. She came to him, and he slept with her. (She had purified herself from her uncleanness.) Then she went back home. The woman conceived and sent word to David, saying, "I am pregnant."

So David sent this word to Joab: "Send me Uriah the Hittite." And Joab sent him to David. When Uriah came to him, David asked him how Joab was, how the soldiers were and how the war was going. Then David said to Uriah, "Go down to your house and wash your feet." So Uriah left the palace, and a gift from the king was sent after him. But Uriah slept at the entrance to the palace with all his master's servants and did not go down to his house.

When David was told, "Uriah did not go home," he asked him, "Haven't you just come from a distance? Why didn't you go home?"

Uriah said to David, "The ark and Israel and Judah are staying in tents, and my master Joab and my lord's men are camped in the open fields. How could I go to my house and eat and drink and lie with my wife? As surely as you live, I will not do such a thing!"

Then David said to him, "Stay here one more day and I will send you back." So Uriah remained in Jerusalem that day and the next. At David's invitation, he ate and drank with him, and David made him drunk. But in the evening Uriah went out to sleep on his mat among his master's servants; he did not go home.

In the morning David wrote a letter to Joab and sent it with Uriah. In it he wrote, "Put Uriah in the front line where the fighting is the fiercest. Then withdraw from him so he will be struck down and die."

So while Joab had the city under siege, he put Uriah at a place where he knew the strongest defenders were. When the men of the city came out and fought against Joab, some of the men in David's army fell, including Uriah the Hittite.

Joab sent David a full account of the battle. He instructed the messenger: "When you have finished giving the king this account of the battle, the king's anger may flare up and he may ask you, 'Why did you get so close to the city to fight? Didn't you know they would shoot arrows from the wall? Who killed Abimelech son of Jerub-Besheth? Didn't a woman throw an upper millstone on him from the wall, so that he died in Thebez?' If he asks you this, then say to him, 'Also, your servant Uriah is dead.' "

The messenger set out, and when he arrived he told David everything Joab had sent him to say. The messenger said to David, "The men overpowered us and came out against us in the open, but we drove them back to the entrance to the city gate. Then the archers shot arrows at your servants from the wall, and some of the king's men died. Moreover, your servant Uriah the Hittite is dead."

David told the messenger, "Say this to Joab: 'Don't let this upset you; the sword devours one as well as another. Press the attack against the city and destroy it.' Say this to encourage Joab."

When Uriah's wife heard that her husband was dead, she mourned for him. After the time of mourning was over, David had her brought to his house, and she became his wife and bore him a son. But the thing David had done displeased the Lord.[2]

Discussion Questions

1. King David placed desire above duty. Uriah placed duty above desire. Consider the quotation of Dr. Szasz given in the introduction to this story: "The quality of our life depends largely on the concordance or discordance between our desires and duties." Do you agree with Dr. Szasz's analysis? Can you think of a time when you were torn between desire and duty? Which did you choose and what do you think of the choice you made?
2. Joab was obedient to King David's order to place Uriah where the fighting was fiercest and then withdraw. Joab's obedience was his expression of loyalty to the king. Do you think Joab should have disobeyed the order to orchestrate Uriah's killing?
3. How do you account for Uriah's loyalty as shown by his refusal to enjoy his wife while his fellow soldiers remained in the field? Do you attribute this to his training as a soldier or something else?

Suggested Follow-Up

1. The movie *A Few Good Men* provides an excellent opportunity to study duty and following orders in the context of the military. Consider viewing this well-written, superbly acted drama starring Kevin Bacon, Tom Cruise, Demi Moore, and Jack Nicholson.[3]
2. Assign II Samuel 12 and Psalm 51 for an account of the aftermath of King David's adultery and subsequent cover-up. This material can be discussed theologically, psychologically, or both. Discuss with

students their thoughts concerning the events described in II Samuel 12 and Psalm 51.

3. Assign an essay in which the students are required to respond to the following question: Is "I was merely following orders" an adequate explanation for any behavior? Orient students to this assignment by informing them about the defense of the Nazi war criminals at Nuremberg, atomic bombings of Hiroshima and Nagasaki, and Vietnam War's My Lai massacre. Each of these cases involved soldiers following orders. Also include in the orientation the line from Tennyson's *The Charge of the Light Brigade*: "Ours is not to reason why, ours is but to do and die."

Chapter XIV

Perseverance

CUTTING AND RUNNING

If you can force your heart and nerve and sinew
To serve your turn long after they are gone
And so hold on when there is nothing left in you
Except the will which says to them "hold on"

Rudyard Kipling

In 2003 columnist Rick Reilly wrote two stories that appeared in Sports Il-
lustrated within weeks of each other. The first described a press conference
at which twenty-seven-year-old Aron Ralston spoke about the self-ampu-
tation of his right arm. The second featured Ben Comen, a South Carolina
high school cross-country runner who has finished last in every race in
which he has competed. Ben Comen has cerebral palsy. Aron Ralston and
Ben Comen not only exemplify perseverance, they are exemplary of it.

When my daughter was a little girl, we played a game with language. I would say to her, "Rachel, say something that no one has ever said before." She would respond with statements like, "Stop eating that bus!" and, "Can you juggle your ears?" I thought of that game when I first heard about Aron Ralston. Certainly, he was the first person to say, "I cut off my right arm with a pocket knife."

Trapped in a Utah cave when an 800-pound boulder shifted and pinned his arm against the cave's wall, after five days of futility he decided to do the only thing that would save his life. Neither his self-surgery nor his description of it was delicate. At a press conference he described the three step procedure of cutting (flesh, muscle, and tendons), breaking (ulna and radius bones), and snipping (nerve). Weakened by a forty-five pound weight loss, Aron Ralston persisted at the amputation that saved his life.

As an athlete Ben Comen has provided us with a riddle: How could America's slowest high school cross-country runner also be the best known? The answer is when he is featured in *Sports Illustrated* because of his persistence. Cerebral palsy is a congenital disorder of the central nervous system characterized by spastic paralysis and defective motor functioning. Ben has cerebral palsy. While it does not impair him intellectually (he is an excellent student), it has a devastating effect on his cross-country time. Unable to complete the three-mile course without falling numerous times and impaired in his ability to get up after falling, Ben's fifty-minute performances have placed him last in every race he has run. Typically, the first-place time in a high school meet is between sixteen-and-a-half and nineteen-and-a-half minutes for boys. Ben always finished twenty minutes behind the second from last runner. But he always finished!

In addition to crossing the finish line with cuts and abrasions, Ben was accompanied by admiring teammates who ran back to join him after they had completed the course. Spectators knew the race was not over until Ben crossed the finish line. They always waited for him, all of them applauding, most of them cheering, and a few of them crying.

Motivation is the inner drive that initiates and sustains activity. Like the wind, it is a force that cannot be seen and is inferred from its effect. Aron Ralston's motivation was to survive. Ben Comen's motivation is not as obvious. Perhaps perseverance has become a way of life for Ben. Perhaps his drive comes from the desire to experience the exhilaration that comes from prevailing in a challenge. Each in his own way serves as an illustration of extraordinary persistence. We admire Aron Ralston because he took control in his circumstances. In his press conference he said that after days of despair it actually felt good to realize that he could do something. Convinced that he was going to die and not knowing when his body would be found, he etched his name into the wall of the cave for the purpose of identification. Ironically, it was when he used his knife for this epitaphic task that it occurred to him that he could also use it to free himself. He was encouraged by the realization that the 800-pound boulder would not determine the time and place of his death.

Similarly, Ben Comen fought back. His adversary was not a boulder but a formidable disease. Like Aron, he resolved not to be held in place. Avoidance of pain is a primal human impulse. Both of these young men are admirable for having persevered through pain to achieve a greater good. They provoke us to wonder if there is anything we so value that would enable us to endure pain. They move us to ask, "Could I find in myself what Ben Comen and Aron Ralston have found in themselves?"

Discussion Questions

1. It has been said, "Heroes are not born, they are cornered." Aron Ralston was "cornered" in a life-and-death situation. This was not the case with Ben Comen. What are some other ways in which their situations differed?
2. Ben Comen did not compete to win races. What accounts for his ability to engage in an activity without excelling at it? Do you have any activities that you enjoy without excelling at them? If so, how do you explain your ability to do so?
3. Psychiatrist Thomas Szasz has written: "People often say that this person or that person has not yet found himself. But the self is not something that one finds; it is something one creates."[1] Do you agree that the self is not found, but created? Assuming Dr. Szasz is correct, what "self" have Aron Ralston and Ben Comen created for themselves?

Suggested Follow-Up

1. Assign a "Where are they now?" assignment. It might be interesting to have an update of Aron and Ben.
2. Aron Ralston has written a book, appropriately titled, *Between a Rock and a Hard Place*.[2] Some students might be interested in knowing more about his story. Part of his survival story is the inventory he took before severing his arm. He said he considered the things he enjoyed and realized that only piano playing required two arms. Talking with students about Aron's pre-amputation inventory might make for an interesting discussion.

Chapter XV

Responsibility

EXPLODING PINTOS

Triggers are pulled by individuals. Orders are given and executed by individuals. In the last analysis, every single human act is ultimately the result of an individual choice.

–Scott Peck

Product liability lawsuits occur when there is a claim that a manufacturer is responsible for injury or damage caused by a product. Of course, it would be ridiculous to hold the manufacturer of a hunting rifle responsible for a murder if the rifle was used in a homicide. However, if the rifle backfired and killed the hunter using it then it is likely that the manufacturer would face a product liability lawsuit.

Perhaps the most famous of these cases is the one that involved the Ford Pinto, an American subcompact car introduced by the Ford Motor Company in 1971 and produced until 1980. The following essay provides an opportunity to discuss corporate responsibility.

When it appeared in 1971, Ford Pinto sales were so brisk that the plain, but fuel-efficient subcompact car was dubbed, "the car nobody loves, but everybody buys." Before its ten-year production run was over, it became "the barbeque that seats four." What happened to this affordable little car that reduced it from popularity to a punchline?

(In the movie "Speed" Sandra Bullock's character, Annie, described driving a bomb-laden bus as, "just like driving a really big Pinto.") Twenty-seven deaths in Pinto collision fires and subsequent product liability suits are what happened.

> Critics argued that the vehicles' lack of a true rear bumper
> as well as any reinforcing structure between the rear panel
> and the rear panel, meant that in certain conditions, the tank
> would be thrust forward into the differential, which had a
> number of protruding bolts that could puncture the tank.
> This, and the fact that doors could potentially jam during
> an accident (due to poor reinforcing) made the car a
> potential deathtrap.[1]

By the time the 1991 *Grimshaw v. Ford Motor Company* product liability case was litigated, *Forbes Magazine* had included the Pinto on its list of the ten worst cars of all time. In the years following there appeared law review papers arguing that the case against Ford was less clear-cut than first believed.[2] Unfortunately for Ford, these papers have received very little attention outside of law school classes, leaving the Pinto with an infamous reputation in automobile history.

The well publicized Pinto collision explosions combined with the movie "Class Action" educated the American public in the practice of *cost-benefit analysis*. In a cost-benefit analysis the expense of an automobile's feature is weighed against the profit or loss it would produce. For example, the expense of adding reinforcement to a car's doors to make it a safer vehicle might increase the sticker price enough to reduce sales. Another type of cost-benefit analysis has sinister implications. It is the calculation of the expense of a recall for a safety concern compared to the cost of anticipated litigation and lawsuit settlements. It was never established that Ford knew the Pinto was prone to collision explosions and decided to let the accidents happen rather than have a recall. However, the media and urban myth combined to give the impression that Ford did make that calculation.

Although a misperception, it raises the ethical question, "Would it have been morally wrong if Ford knew about the Pinto's problem but decided against a recall as a result of a cost-benefit analysis?"

The philosopher Immanuel Kant wrote: "Act so that you treat humanity, whether in your own person or in that of another, always as an end and never as a means only."[3] Kant believed that because nothing is more valuable than human beings, ethical decisions should always reflect what is best for them. Kant would say that where human life is concerned a cost-benefit analysis is unnecessary. He would say that if a recall would have saved even a single life then it should have occurred.

The following argument could be made against Kant's position: The decision-makers at the Ford Motor Company have a responsibility to the stockholders. It is the responsibility to maximize company profit. Caring for humanity is not part of the decision-makers' job description. Kant is free to put people first in his own affairs, but he has no authority to impose his moral standard on others.

Discussion Questions

1. Of course, the twenty-seven deaths referred to in this essay are tragic. However, do you think this is an unusually high number for the two-million Pintos produced from 1971 to 1980?
2. Do you agree with Immanuel Kant's hypothetical advice to the Ford Motor Company or the argument against Kant?
3. Consider the quotation of Dr. Scott Peck that introduces this essay. Does his analysis of responsibility imply that people are responsible not only for what they do, but also for what they fail to do? If so, does this mean that anyone at the Ford Motor Company who suspected the Pinto was an unsafe car had a responsibility to report this to the company? What if a worker did report this and the company did not take action? Would that relieve the worker of responsibility?

Suggested Follow-Up

1. Assign students to ask a number of people who are forty-five or older: "What comes to mind when you hear *Ford Pinto*?" Compare your students' findings with the facts presented in this essay and report this comparison back to the students.
2. Watch the climactic courtroom scene from the movie, "Class Action" starring Gene Hackman.[4] This scene is approximately fifteen minutes in length and within the last twenty minutes of the movie. It is not the true story of the Ford Pinto, but is obviously inspired by it. After seeing this scene, discuss the difference between the movie and

the actual Pinto case. Include in the discussion the influence of movies
on people's perceptions and misperceptions of historical events.

ADDICTION AND RESPONSIBILITY

To be a man, a woman, an adult, is to accept responsibility.
                                           –Antoine de Saint-Exupery

I recommend that the Statue of Liberty on the East Coast be supplemented
by a Statue of Responsibility on the West Coast.
                                           –Viktor Frankl

Responsibility is the fact of being obligated to do something and/or an-
swer to someone. It requires self-discipline, the ability to do what ought
to be done regardless of mood. Responsible people are able to separate
their obligations from those of other people. Taking responsibility also
means taking action. The "Prayer for Serenity," "Autobiography in Five
Short Chapters," and the story of the alcoholic sergeant speak to the ne-
cessities of recognizing, accepting, and acting on responsibilities.

What makes people responsible for their behavior? In the summer of
2001 Andrea Yates, the mother of five children ranging in age from six
months to seven years, drowned them—one after the other—in a bath-
tub. The psychiatric evaluation for her unspeakable act was her chronic
depression complicated by psychotic episodes. It was during one of
Mrs. Yates departures from reality and under the influence of an audi-
tory hallucination that she accomplished the murders of her children.

In 1848 a Vermont railroad worker miraculously survived an explosion in which a three-and-a-half foot iron rod entered at his left cheek-
bone, passed through his brain, and exited through the top of his skull.
The man, Phineas Gage, went from being a reliable crew foreman to,
"an animal in a man's body" as one of his co-workers characterized
him. The medical explanation for Gage's loss of impulse control was
the separation of his brain's limbic system, which fires impulses, from
its frontal cortex, which restrains impulses.

On May 27, 2006 an Illinois physician threw his eight and four-year-old sons from the fifteenth floor balcony of the hotel where they were vacationing. Dr. Edward Van Dyke then followed his sons over the railing by jumping to his own death, making an explanation of this bizarre murder-suicide unlikely.

Andrea Yates, Phineas Gage, and Edward Van Dyke—what makes people responsible for their behavior? In each of these tragedies there is the implication of mental defect. *Insanity* is not a psychological term but a legal expression. In the United States there is no single definition of insanity agreed upon by all jurisdictions. However, the various definitions imply that an insane person is either incapable of distinguishing right from wrong behavior or lacks the ability to resist an impulse to act.

In the ordinary circumstances of life, people are held responsible for actions correctly assigned to them that are within their control. A fourteen-year-old boy who is responsible for taking out the trash is obligated to accomplish a chore of which he is aware and capable.

The failure of one person to meet a responsibility does not necessarily make that obligation transferable to another. For example, an employee might refuse the request of a co-worker with the words, "Your failure to plan doesn't become my responsibility!"

Sometimes a responsibility can be so dispersed that it goes unrecognized and no action is taken. In 1964 a New York woman, Kitty Genovese, was stabbed to death in the parking lot outside of her apartment building. Adding to this tragedy is that thirty-eight people living in the apartment building heard her screams but did nothing to help. If just one of them had called the police, her murder could have been prevented since the attacker twice left her and then returned to stab her again to make certain that she was dead. The time between the first and third attacks was a half-hour.

The "Prayer for Serenity," attributed to theologian Rienhold Niebuhr, provides guidance for discerning responsibility. It begins with, "God grant me serenity to accept the things I cannot change, courage to change the things I can, and wisdom to know the difference." This prayer is recited at every AA (Alcoholics Anonymous) meeting, a place where those who have taken responsibility for their addiction gather to support one another in their recovery. In contrast to them is the army sergeant described in psychiatrist Scott Peck's book, *The Road Less Traveled.* The sergeant was in trouble because of

his excessive drinking and was referred to Dr. Peck for evaluation
and, if necessary, treatment.

He denied that he was an alcoholic or
that his use of alcohol was a personal problem, saying, "There's
nothing else to do in Okinawa in the evenings except drink."
"Do you like to read," I asked.
"Oh yes, I like to read, sure."
"Then why don't you read in the evening instead of drinking?"
"It's too noisy to read in the barracks."
"Well then, why don't you go to the library?"
"The library is too far away."
"Is the library farther away than the bar you go to?"
"Well, I'm not much of a reader. That's not where my interests
lie."
"Do you like to fish," I then inquired.
"Sure, I love to fish."
"Why not go fishing instead of drinking?"
"Because I have to work all day long."
"Can't you go fishing at night?"
"No, there isn't any night fishing in Okinawa."
"But there is, " I said. "I know several organizations that fish at
night here. Would you like me to put you in touch with them?
"Well, I really don't like to fish."
"What I hear you saying, " I clarified, "is that there are other things
to do in Okinawa except drink, but the thing you like to do most in
Okinawa is drink."
"Yeah, I guess so."
"But your drinking is getting you in trouble, so you're faced with a
real problem, aren't you?"
"This damn island would drive anyone to drink."
I kept trying for a while, but the sergeant was not the least bit
interested in seeing his drinking as a personal problem which he could
solve either with or without help, and I regretfully told his commander
that he was not amenable to assistance. His drinking continued, and he
was separated from the service in mid-career.[1]

In contrast to Andrea Yates, Phineas Gage, and Dr. Van Dyke, there
is no indication of a mental defect with the sergeant. He is aware that
his drinking is threatening his career and help is available to him. With
neither psychosis nor head injury impairing his judgment, he is respon-

sible for his excessive drinking. This does not mean that it will be easy for him to bring his drinking under control. The following allegory describes the arduous process of addiction recovery.

Autobiography in Five Short Chapters

I

I walk down the street. There is a deep hole in the sidewalk.
I fall in. I am lost ... I am helpless ...It isn't my fault. It takes me forever to find a way out.

II

I walk down the same street. There is a deep hole in the sidewalk.
I pretend I don't see it. I fall in, again. I can't believe I'm in this same place. But, it isn't my fault. It still takes a long time to get out.

III

I walk down the same street. There is a deep hole in the sidewalk.
I <u>see</u> it is there. I still fall in ... it's a habit ... but, my eyes are open.
I know where I am. It <u>is</u> my fault. I get out immediately.

IV

I walk down the same street. There is a deep hole in the sidewalk.
I walk around it.

V

I walk down another street.

–Anonymous

Note the healthy progression in this autobiography. By recognizing and taking control of a behavior that can be controlled ("I walk down another street.") the sequence that culminates in the addictive behavior ("I fall in.") is not allowed to begin. Taking responsibility for what *cannot* be controlled requires taking responsibility for the preliminary behaviors that *can* be controlled.

Conclusion

Socrates and others theorized that what is commonly referred to as *sin* is actually *ignorance* — ignorance of the damaging effect of irresponsible behavior. A goal of psychotherapy is to enable clients to see how their failure to take responsibility for their behavior impedes them from reaching their stated goals and desires. If we could realize how our failures to be responsible sabotage our own happiness we would be more responsible people.

Discussion Questions

1. Psychiatrist Thomas Szasz has written, "The proverb warns that, 'You should not bite the hand that feeds you.' But maybe you should, if it prevents you from feeding yourself."[2] What is Dr. Szasz saying about helping others with their responsibilities?
2. What do you believe about the *insanity plea* as used in cases like the Andrea Yates murders?
3. In this essay it is implied that the thirty-eight witnesses to Kitty Genovese's murder had a responsibility to do something. Do you agree that they were obligated to act? Why or why not?

Suggested Follow-Up

1. An allegory is a symbolic representation. In a literary allegory the subject described in words stands for a deeper reality. In "Autobiography in Five Short Chapters" the subject is coping with the hole in the sidewalk. Discuss some well-known allegorical works and why an allegory is an effective means of instruction.
2. After discussing allegories, assign the writing of an allegory.

GOING CRAZY IN TEXAS—A TEEN'S AFFAIR (ABIGAIL VAN BUREN)

Your head's a bad neighborhood: Don't go there alone … Empty yourself of self, then kneel down to listen.

–Mary Karr

Reviving Ophelia *is psychologist Mary Pipher's bestselling book about her work with troubled adolescent girls. She wrote that one of her goals for her clients is a "realistic appraisal of their environment." In addition, she seeks to, "help clients see things in new ways and develop richer, more rewarding relationships" and realize that, "the ideal life is calm, fun, and responsible." After reading the following letter to Dear Abby from a fifteen-year-old girl, you might agree that she would benefit from being one of Dr. Pipher's clients.[1]*

Dear Abby:

I am fifteen years old and have a big problem. "Whitney," 17, and I have been friends for a long time. Her boyfriend, "Josh," 21, broke up with her. Soon after, Josh and I started talking. I really liked him. He was cool, and we had a lot of fun.

When Whitney found out Josh and I were hooking up, she got jealous. One night when I was with Josh, Whitney called my parents and told them where I was. I had told my parents I was with another girlfriend.

My father got angry and went on and on for about a week questioning me about my relationship with Josh. When I couldn't stand it anymore I admitted we were having sex. Father called the police and had Josh arrested. He was charged with child molestation.

I told the detective I had lied about Josh and me having sex, but he didn't believe me. Josh was found guilty of statutory rape and sent to prison for five years. The court wouldn't allow me to testify.

My life is over. My former friends hate me. They call me names and write me dirty notes threatening revenge. Josh was popular and has a lot of friends.

I want to help Josh get out of prison. He did not rape me. I knew exactly what I was doing. I have had sex with boys for about two years, but my parents don't know. I'm afraid if I tell them, they'll have those other boys arrested too.

Josh does not deserve to be in prison. What can I do to make up for what has happened because Whitney got jealous and got us into trouble? Please don't tell me to talk to a school counselor. Everyone at school hates me.

- Going Crazy in Texas

Discussion Questions

1. Here is Dear Abby's response to "Going Crazy in Texas:"

Dear Going Crazy:

Regardless of your sexual history, at 21, Josh was old enough to know better. He was sneaking around with a minor—you—and in doing so he broke the law.

It's time for you to grow up and stop blaming others for a problem you caused. If you won't go to a school counselor, contact a local mental health clinic and ask for teen counseling. And since there is hostility at your high school, perhaps you should consider transferring and finishing your education at another school.

Discussion Questions

1. What do you think of Dear Abby's response?
2. Consider the following statements from the girl's letter: (1) "My life is over." (2) "I knew exactly what I was doing." (3) "Josh does not deserve to be in prison." Do you think they are accurate assessments on her part?
3. What do you think of the judge's ruling in giving Josh a five-year sentence?
4. What do you think of the action taken by "Going Crazy's" father?

Suggested Follow-Up

1. Invite a lawyer to discuss with your class the legal issue of statutory rape.
2. Invite a mental health professional to discuss with your class the psychological implications of sex at an early age.

Chapter XVI

Thoughtfulness

ON EDUCATION AND E.T. (PETER KREEFT)

The unexamined life is not worth living.

–Socrates

Thoughtfulness can mean either kind or contemplative. When Socrates said, "The unexamined life is not worth living," he meant that the richest life available is a life lived thoughtfully. According to Socrates, contemplation of why we think, act, and feel as we do adds value to our lives.

In his witty and insightful book, The Best Things in Life, *philosopher Peter Kreeft places Socrates on a contemporary college campus, Desperate State University.[1] There Socrates has a series of conversations with the students and professors he finds there. The first of these interactions is with Peter Pragma, a student who seems to be living an unexamined life.*

Socrates: Excuse me for bothering you, but what are you doing?

Peter: What kind of silly question is that? I'm reading a book. Or was, until you interrupted me. Can't you see that?

Socrates: Alas, I often fail to see what others see, and see things others cannot see.

Peter: I don't get it.

Socrates: I saw you holding the book, yes, but I did not see you reading it.

Peter: What in the world are you talking about?

Socrates: You are holding the book in your hands, aren't you?

Peter: Of course.

Socrates: And I can see your hands.

Peter: So?

Socrates: But do you read the book with your hands?

Peter: Of course not.

Socrates: With what, then?

Peter: With my eyes, of course.

Socrates: Oh, I don't think so.

Peter: I think you're crazy.

Socrates: Perhaps, but I speak the truth, and I think I can show you that. Tell me, can a corpse read?

Peter: No ...

Socrates: But a corpse can have eyes, can't it?

Peter: Yes.

Socrates: Then it is not just the eyes that read.

Peter: Oh. The mind then. Are you satisfied now?

Socrates: No.

Peter: Somehow I thought you'd say that.

Socrates: I cannot see your mind, can I?

Peter: No.

Socrates: Then I cannot see you reading.

Peter: I guess you can't. But what a strange thing to say!

Socrates: Strange but true. Truth is often stranger than fiction, you know. Which do you prefer?

Peter: You know, you're stranger than fiction too, little man.

Socrates: That's because I'm true too.

Peter: Who are you, anyway?

Socrates: I am Socrates.

Peter: Sure you are. And I'm E.T.

Socrates: I'm pleased to meet you, E.T.

Peter: My name is Peter Pragma.

Socrates: Do you have two names?

Peter: What do you mean?

Socrates: You said your name was E.T.

Peter: And you said your name was Socrates.

Socrates: Because it is. I have this strange habit of saying what is.

Peter: What do you want from me?

Socrates: Would you let me pursue my silly question just a moment longer?

Peter: I thought you got your answer.

Socrates: Not to my real question. You see, when I asked you what you were doing, I really meant *why* are you doing it?

Peter: I'm studying for my exam tomorrow.

Socrates: And why are you doing *that*?

Peter: You know, you sound like a little child.

Socrates: Thank you.

Peter: I didn't mean it as a compliment.

Socrates: I don't care. Only answer the question, please.

Peter: I'm studying to pass my course, of course.

Socrates: And why do you want to do that?

Peter: Another silly question! Don't you ever grow up?

Socrates: Let me tell you a secret, Peter: There *are* no grown-ups. But you still haven't answered my "silly question."

Peter: To get a degree, of course.

Socrates: You mean all the time and effort and money you put into your education here at Desperate State is to purchase that little piece of paper?

Peter: That's the way it is.

Socrates: I think you may be able to guess what the next question is going to be.

Peter: I'm catching on. I think it's an infection.

Socrates: What is the next question, then?

Peter: You're going to ask me why I want a degree.

Socrates: And you're going to answer.

Peter: But it's another silly question. Everyone knows what a degree is for.

Socrates: But I am not "everyone." So would you please tell me?

Peter: A college degree is the entrance ticket to a good job. Do you know how difficult the job market is today? Where have you been for the last few years?

Socrates: You wouldn't believe me if I told you. But we must ask just one more question, or rather two: What is a "good job" and why do you want one?

Peter: Money, of course. That's the answer to both questions. To all questions, maybe.

Socrates: I see. And what do you want to do with all the money you make?

Peter: You said your last two questions were your last.

Socrates: If you want to go away, I cannot keep you here. But if we pursue our explorations one little step further, we may discover something new.

Peter: What do you think you'll find? A new world?

Socrates: Quite possibly. A new world of thought. Will you come with me? Shall we trudge ahead through the swamps of our uncertainties? Or shall we sit comfortably at home in our little cave?

Peter: Why should I torture myself with all these silly questions from a strange little man? I'm supposed to be studying for my exam.

Socrates: Because it would be profitable for you. The unexamined life is not worth living, you know.

Peter: I heard that somewhere ... Good grief! That's one of the quotations that might be on my exam tomorrow. Who said that, anyway?

Socrates: I did. Didn't you hear me?

Peter: No, I mean who said it originally?

Socrates: It was I, I assure you. Now shall we continue our journey?

Peter: What are you getting at, anyway, Socrates?

Socrates: No, Peter, the question is what are *you* getting at? That is the topic we were exploring. Now shall we continue to make your life a little less unexamined and a little more worth living?

Peter: All right. For a little while, anyway.

Socrates: Then you will answer my last question?

Peter: I forgot what it was.

Socrates: What do you need money for?

Peter: Everything! Everything I want costs money.

Socrates: For instance?

Peter: Do you know how much it costs to raise a family nowadays?

Socrates: And what would you say is the largest expense in raising a family nowadays?

Peter: Probably sending the kids to college.

Socrates: I see. Let's review what you have said. You are reading this book to study for your exam, so that you can pass it and your course, to graduate and get a degree, to get a good job, to make a lot of money, to raise a family and send your children to college.

Peter: Right.

Socrates: And why will they go to college?

Peter: Same reason I'm here. To get good jobs, of course.

Socrates: So they can send their children to college?

Peter: Yes.

Socrates: Have you ever heard the expression "arguing in a circle"?

Peter: No, I never took logic.

Socrates: Really? I never would have guessed it.

Peter: You're teasing me.

Socrates: Really?

Peter: I'm a practical man. I don't care about logic, just life.

Socrates: Then perhaps we should call what you are doing "living in a circle." Have you ever asked yourself a terrifying, threatening question? What is the whole circle there for?

Peter: Hmmm ... nobody ever bothered me with that question before.

Socrates: I know. That is why I was sent to you.

Peter: Well, sending kids to college isn't the only thing I'm working for. I'm working for my own good to. That's not a circle, is it?

Socrates: We don't know until we look, do we? Tell me, what is "your own good"?

Peter: What do you mean?

Socrates: What benefit to yourself do you hope the money from a well-paying job will bring you?

Peter: All sorts of things. The good life. Fun and games. Leisure.

Socrates: I see. And you are now giving up fun and games for some serious studying so you can pass your exams and your courses and get your degree.

Peter: Right. It's called "delayed gratification." I could be watching the football game now, or playing poker. But I'm putting my time in the bank. It's an investment for the future. You see, when I'm set up in a good job, I'll be able to call my own shots.

Socrates: You mean you will then have leisure and be able to watch football games or play poker whenever you wish.

Peter: Right.

Socrates: Why don't you just do those things right now?

Peter: What?

Socrates: Why do you work instead of play if all you want to do is play? You're working now so that years from now you can have enough money to afford leisure to play. But you can play now. So why take the long, hard road if you're already home? It seems to be another circle back to where you started from, where you are now.

Peter: Are you telling me I should just drop out of school and goof off?

Socrates: No. I am telling you that you should find a good reason to be here. I don't think you have found that yet. Shall we keep searching?

Peter: All right, wise man or wise guy, whichever you are. You tell me. Why should I be here? What's the value of college? You've got a sermon up your sleeve, haven't you?

Socrates: Is that what you expect me to do?

Peter: Sure. Didn't you just tear down my answers so that you could sell me yours?

Socrates: Indeed not. I am not a wise man, only a philosopher, a lover and pursuer of wisdom, that divine but elusive goal.

Peter: What do you want with me then?

Socrates: To spread the infection of philosophizing.

Peter: So you're not going to teach me the answers?

Socrates: No. I think the most valuable lesson I could teach you is to become your own teacher. Isn't that one of the things you are here to learn? Isn't that one of the greatest values of a college education? Have none of your teachers taught you that?

What has become of my great invention, anyway?

Peter: I guess I never looked at education that way.

Socrates: It's not too late to begin.

Peter: It is today, Socrates—or whoever you are. I'm really too busy today.

Socrates: Too busy to know why you're so busy? Too busy doing to know what you're doing?

Peter: Look, maybe we could continue this conversation some other time. I have more important things to do than this stuff ...

Socrates: Philosophy. His stuff is philosophy. What exam are you studying for, by the way?

Peter: Well, actually, it's a philosophy exam.

Socrates: I see. I think you may be in trouble there.

Peter: No way. I've memorized the professors notes. I've got all the answers.

Socrates: And none of the questions. What is the value of your answers then?

Peter: I just can't waste my time on questions like that.

Socrates: Because you have to study philosophy?

Peter: Yes. Good-bye, strange little man.

Socrates: Good-bye, E.T. I hope some day you escape your circular wanderings and find your way home.

Discussion Questions

1. The "Socratic Method" is the technique of teaching by asking questions. What do you think Socrates saw in this method that made him believe it was effective?
2. Have you experienced any teachers who employ the "Socratic Method?"

Suggested Follow-Up

1. Stephen Vincent Benet wrote: "Life is not lost by dying! Life is lost minute by minute, day by dragging day, in all the thousand, small, uncaring ways."[2] Assign a brief essay in which students are asked to analyze this quotation and apply it to Peter Pragma.
2. Peter Kreeft's *The Best Things in Life* is a thought provoking book that is fun to read and discuss.[3] Consider assigning this book. It is 187 pages in length.

Chapter XVII

Wisdom

PAPA, THE EDUCATOR (LEONARD BUSCAGLIA)

I never allowed school to interfere with my education.

−Mark Twain

In the 1980's Leonard Buscaglia, Professor of Education at the University of Southern California, was one of America's best known lecturers and widely read writers. His bestselling books include Loving Each Other *and* Living, Loving, and Learning. *One of his lesser-known books is* Papa, My Father.[1] *Although not formally educated, Papa Buscaglia loved learning and appreciated how it enriches one's life. The story, "Papa, the Educator" describes a man of uncommon discernment and sound judgment—two characteristics of one who is wise.*

"There is so much to learn," he'd remind us. Though we're born stupid, only the stupid remain that way ." To ensure that none of his children ever fell into the trap of complacency, he insisted that we learn at least one new thing each day. He felt that there could be no fact too insignificant, that each bit of learning made us more of a person and insured us against boredom and stagnation.

So Papa devised a ritual. Since dinnertime was family time and everyone came to dinner unless they were dying of malaria, it seemed the perfect forum for sharing what new things we had learned that day. Of course, as children we thought this was perfectly crazy. There was

99

no doubt, when we compared such paternal concerns with other children's fathers that Papa was weird.

It would never have occurred to us to deny Papa a request. So when my brother and sisters and I congregated in the bathroom to clean up for dinner, the inevitable question was, "What did *you* learn today?" If the answer was "Nothing," we didn't dare sit at the table without first finding a fact in our much-used encyclopedia. "The population of Nepal...," etc.

Now, thoroughly clean and armed with our fact for the day, we were ready for dinner. I can still see the table piled high with mountains of food. So large were the mounds of pasta that as a boy I was often unable to see my sister sitting across from me. (The pungent aromas were such that, over a half century later, even in memory they cause me to salivate.)

Dinner was noisy time of clattering dishes and endless activity. It was also a time to review the activities of the day. Our animated conversations were always conducted in Piedmontese dialect since Mama didn't speak English. The events we recounted, no matter how insignificant, were never taken lightly. Mama and Papa always listened carefully and were ready with some comment, often profound and analytical, always right to the point.

"That was the smart thing to do." "*Stupido*, how could you be so dumb?" "*Cosi sia,* you deserved it." "*E allora*, no one is perfect." "*Testa dura* ('hardhead'), you should have known better. Didn't we teach you anything?" "Oh, that's nice." One dialogue ended and immediately another began. Silent moments were rare at our table.

Then came the grand finale to every meal, the moment we dreaded most—the time to share the day's new learning. The mental imprint of those sessions still runs before me like a familiar film clip, vital and vivid.

Papa, at the head of the table, would push his chair back slightly, a gesture that signified the end of the eating and suggested that there would be a new activity. He would pour a small glass of red wine, light up a thin, potent Italian cigar, inhale deeply, exhale, then take stock of his family.

For some reason this always had a slightly unsettling effect on us as we stared back at Papa, waiting for him to say something. Every so often he would explain why he did this. He told us that if he didn't take time to look at us, we would soon be grown and he would have missed us. So he'd stare at us, one after another.

Finally, his attention would settle upon one of us. "*Felice*," he would say to me, "tell me what you learned today."

"I learned that the population of Nepal is..."

Silence.

It always amazed me, and reinforced my belief that Papa was a little crazy, that nothing I ever said was considered too trivial for him. First, he'd think about what was said as if the salvation of the world depended upon it.

"The population of Nepal. Hmmm. Well."

He would then look down the table at Mama, who would be ritualistically fixing her favorite fruit in a bit of leftover wine. "Mama, did you know that?"

Mama's responses were always astonishing and seemed to lighten the otherwise reverential atmosphere. "Nepal," she'd say. "Nepal? Not only don't I know the population of Nepal, I don't know where in God's world it is!" Of course, this was only playing into Papa's hands.

"*Felice*," he'd say. "Get the atlas so we can show Mama where Nepal is." And the search began. The whole family went on a search for Nepal. This same experience was repeated until each family member had a turn. No dinner at our house ever ended without our having been enlightened by at least a half dozen such facts.

As children, we thought very little about these educational wonders and even less about how we were being enriched. We couldn't have cared less. We were too impatient to have dinner end so we could join our less-educated friends in a rip-roaring game of kick the can.

In retrospect, after years of studying how people learn, I realize what a dynamic educational technique Papa was offering us, reinforcing the value of continual learning. Without being aware of it, our family was growing together, sharing experiences, and participating in one another's education. Papa was, without knowing it, giving us an education in the most real sense. By looking at us, listening to us, hearing us, respecting our opinions, affirming our value, giving us a sense of dignity, he was unquestionably our most influential teacher.

Discussion Questions

1. Professor Buscaglia describes his father as "weird' yet also wrote, "It would never have occurred to us to deny Papa a request." What in

this story helps to explain the mutual respect and affection between Papa and his children?

2. Does dinnertime in your home in any way resemble that of the Buscaglia family? Does your family have any rituals at dinnertime upon which either or both of your parents insist?

3. Felice (Professor Buscaglia) grew up to be a professor of education. What do you think he learned about teaching from his father? (Hint: It might be helpful to reread the last paragraph of the story).

Suggested Follow-Up

Solomon, the king of Israel, is a name associated with wisdom. In fact, his name has taken the form of an adjective (solomonic) and is used to characterize extraordinary wisdom. In the Hebrew Bible (Old Testament) historical book First Kings (Chapter 3, Verses 16-28) is a well-known story in which King Solomon's wisdom is demonstrated. After reading it, discuss how it is a story that illustrates wisdom. Also, discuss the difference between wisdom and intelligence.

THE PARABLE OF SHLOMO

A fool finds no pleasure in understanding, but delights in airing his own opinions.

- Proverbs 18:2

Knowledge, intelligence, and wisdom are not synonymous. People who are knowledgeable are well-informed, having accumulated much information. Intelligent people acquire information and understanding with ease. People who are wise have soundness of judgment. Wisdom is the ability to distinguish right from wrong and discern truth.

Parables are stories that illustrate moral principles. The "Parable of Shlomo" is not a story about archery. It illustrates wisdom by contrast. Shlomo's approach to archery is parallel to the process by which unwise people establish truth.

Once upon a time there was a man sent by his king to recruit archers for the king's army. The man searched far and wide but could not find even one man good enough with a bow-and-arrow to serve the king. Finally, coming upon a small village, the man took delight in what he saw. What he saw were targets painted on the sides of numerous buildings, trees, and hillsides. Especially pleasing to him was that each of the targets had an arrow in the dead center, "bull's eye" location. Excited, he asked the first villager he saw, "Who is the master archer who lives in this village? He is needed for the king's army."

The man of the village responded, "We have no such man in this village!"

The king's agent then asked, "But what about all these targets with arrows in the dead center?"

The villager replied with a laugh, "Oh, those things! Those are from Shlomo, our village idiot. He goes around shooting arrows all over the place and then paints a target around them wherever they land."

Discussion Questions

1. The quotation from Proverbs that introduces the section states in one sentence what the "Parable of Shlomo" illustrates. Can you state in your own words what both the Proverb and the parable are saying about truth?

2. President Clinton is generally viewed as a very intelligent man. He himself admits that he exercised poor judgment by choosing to be involved with Monica Lewinsky. How do you explain a man of superior intelligence showing such a lack of wisdom?

3. Plato divided the mind into three parts: reason, the spirited element, and appetites. Reason is the individual's desire to be rational. The spirited element is the individual's sense of pride or honor. Appetites maintain the body by satisfying the physical cravings for food, drink, sex, etc. Plato taught that wrongdoing occurs when reason and the spirited element fail to control the appetites. A common explanation for this failure is the repetitive indulgence of appetites makes them stronger than reason. If Plato is right, what can people do to bring their appetites under the control of reason? (Another way of asking this question is: How can we conform our behavior to what we say we want it to be so that we can live wisely?)

Suggested Activity

One of Monty Python's best-known skits is the "Dead Parrot Skit" in which a customer and pet shop clerk argue over whether or not a recently purchased parrot is dead. The hilarious skit provides a launching point for a discussion of the difference between *objective* and *subjective* truth. (*Monty Python's And Now For Something Completely Different*, 1981, Columbia Tristar Home Video. Running Time: 88 Minutes.)

A PHILOSOPHER ALMOST COMMITS SUICIDE

Tomorrow and tomorrow and tomorrow creeps in this petty pace from day to day to the last syllable of recorded time...life is but a walking shadow...it is a tale told by an idiot, full of sound and fury, signifying nothing.
                            –William Shakespeare (*Macbeth, Act V, Scene 5*)

From 1951, with the publication of his first book, The True Believer, *to his death in 1983, Eric Hoffer was one of America's best known philosophers. Two years after learning to read in both German and English at age five, Hoffer lost his eyesight in a fall. Inexplicably, he regained his sight at age fifteen. Fearing that he would lose his vision again as suddenly as he regained it, he committed himself to reading as much as he could for as long as he could. Happily, he did not return to blindness. Sixty-six years of reading hours and hours every day made Hoffer a uniquely self-educated man. At age twenty-eight he decided to commit suicide. He changed his mind when the idea for a new life serendipitously occurred to him.*

Eric Hoffer lived frugally; so much so that when he became unemployed at age twenty-eight he projected that he could live on his savings for a year. Instead of looking for work he decided to spend the year figuring out what he would do for the rest of his life. As that year came to a close, he reflected on the routine of his life: sleeping, eating, reading, and studying. He wondered whether it mattered if he died at the end of the year or ten years later. Characteristically, he approached his suicide methodically.

A revolver would have been ideal, but it was not to
be had without a police permit. Gas might leak into
adjoining rooms and alarm the neighbors. Death by
jumping from a bridge or being run over seemed
crude. There remained poison.[1]

Following his research on various poisons and the kind of death each
would bring, Hoffer settled on oxalic acid. A systemic poison, it would
disable his nervous system and bring about unconsciousness - eventually a sleep from which he would never awaken. Frugal to the end, he
purchased a bottle of oxalic acid crystals for twenty-five cents and
walked to an isolated spot at the edge of town. As he ingested the poison, he looked away from the town and down the road he would never
walk. He thought,

It would be good if this street had no end - I would
walk on forever, and my feet would never tire, neither
would I fret nor complain...I did not know then
that the sudden vision of life as an endless road
was the first intimation of a revolt against suicide.[2]

Spitting out the toxic crystals, he turned around and headed back to
town, coughing violently. Later, in a cafeteria, he reevaluated his life.

As I swallowed my food the vision of life as a
Road - a winding, endless road that knows not
where it goes and what its load - came back to
me. Here was an alternative that I had not thought
of to the deadening routine of a workingman's
life in the city. I must get out on the road which
winds from town to town. Each town would be
new. Each town would proclaim itself best and
bid me take my chance. I would take them all
and never repent.
    I did not commit suicide, but on that
Sunday a workingman died and a tramp was
born.[3]

In various ways, wisdom is understood as the ability to make right
moral decisions. A recurring theme in the Hebrew Bible's book of
Proverbs is the contrast between the wise man and the fool. The former

manages his life well by choosing the right path; the latter multiplies his troubles by opting for the wrong ethical course. Was Eric Hoffer's decision to not kill himself an expression of wisdom?

At age twenty-eight Hoffer's life problem was its absence of meaning; its "petty pace from day to day." He solved his problem - perhaps it was solved for him - by the rush of insight that the life he had been living was not the life he was compelled to live. Like the untraveled road stretched out before him, the unexplored years ahead were uncertain. In that inexplicable way in which insight comes in a rush, Hoffer recognized that implicit in the unknown was the possibility of a satisfying life. In that moment the death of a workingman became the birth of a tramp.

Years later Hoffer wrote, "How much easier is self-sacrifice than self-realization."[4] By not ending his life he went on to write *The True Believer*, a "slim volume (which) contains more ideas per page than some entire books."[5] The disciplines of philosophy and literature are the better for Hoffer's self-realization. Was Hoffer the better for living fifty-three years beyond his aborted suicide? From his writing it seems that he was:

> My twenty-five years as a longshoreman were
> a fruitful interval in my life. I learned to write
> and published several books...I write because
> I must. I do not think of myself as a writer.[6]

The writer Walker Percy hyperbolically stated that the sincere contemplation of suicide is necessary for a satisfying life. He posited that it is only when one rejects that he *must* live and embraces that he *chooses* to live that life can be enjoyed. Eric Hoffer chose to live and went on to write, "It is the pull of opposite poles that stretches souls. And only stretched souls make music."[7] Pulled between life and death a half-century before he died, Eric Hoffer made music.

Discussion Questions

1. Do you believe there is such thing as a rational suicide?
2. Mark Twain is credited with the quotation: "I never let school interfere with my education." Certainly, Eric Hoffer exemplifies this quotation. What are your thoughts about the relevancy and usefulness of your education?

3. Hoffer described the day he almost committed suicide as the day "a workingman died and a tramp was born." What did Hoffer mean by these words? (Could his experience be characterized as a born-again experience?)
4. Consider Hoffer's decision to educate himself after he regained his eyesight. Consider what occurred to him after he swallowed the oxalic acid crystals and looked down the road. What do these two decisions have in common?

Suggested Follow-Up

1. Give your students a research assignment calling for further investigation of Eric Hoffer's life and work. (Unfortunately Hoffer's memoir, *Truth Imagined*, is out of print and somewhat difficult to acquire. It is a well-written, interesting read of ninety-seven pages.[8])
2. The Academy Award winning film, "Good Will Hunting" is the story of a self-educated genius. It provides an opportunity to discuss intelligence's limited contribution to a happy, contented life.
3. A book addressing the loss of a friend or loved one to suicide is *Living When a Young Friend Commits Suicide or is Even Thinking About It* (Beacon Press, 1999).[9] Written for teenagers by Earl Grollman and Max Malikow, it is eighty-five pages in length and has a question-and-answer format. It informs about suicide and can generate discussion.

Notes

I. ADAPTABILITY

Blindsided

1. Cohen, Richard, *Blindsided: A Reluctant Memoir* (New York: Harper Collins Publishers, 2004), pp. 22-224.

Tragic Optimism

1. Frankl, Viktor, *Man's Search for Meaning*, (New York: Washington Square Press, 1959), p. 32.
2. Ibid., p. 16.
3. Ibid., p. 131.
4. Ibid., p. 162.
5. Cronkite, Kathy, *On the Edge of Darkness* (New York: Doubleday, 1994), p. 315.
6. Nouwen, Henri, *The Wounded Healer* (Garden City, NY: Image Books, 1979).
7. Frankl, p. 88.
8. Montgomery, Lucy Maude, "The Price," After Many Days (Toronto, Ontario Canada: McClelland and Stewart, Inc., 1991), p. 135.
9. Ibid., p. 141.
10. Frankl, p. 162.
11. Lewis, C.S., *The Problem of Pain: How Human Suffering Raises Almost Intolerable Intellectual Problems* (New York: Macmillan Publishing Co., 1962), p.122.

12. Denton, Jeremiah, *When Hell Was in Session* (Mobile, AL: Denton Associates, Inc., 1982), pp. 58-77.

13. Monroe, Kim, *Finding God at Harvard* (Grand Rapids, MI: Zondervan Press, 1996), p. 130.

14. Trueblood, Elton, *The Life We Prize* (New York: Harper and Row, 1951), p. 130.

15. Frankl, p. 162.

16. Jung, Carl Gustav, *Modern Man in Search of a Soul* (New York: Harcourt Brace Jovanovich, Publishers, 1933), p. 231.

17. Frankl, p. 15.

Abraham Lincoln's Depression

1. Shenk, Joshua Wolf, "Lincoln's Great Depression," *The Atlantic Monthly*, October 2005, p. 56.

2. Myers, David, *Psychology*, eighth edition (New York: Worth Publishers, 2004), pp. 633-634.

3. Styron, William, *Darkness Visible: A Memoir of Madness* (New York: Vintage Books, 1990), p. 37.

4. Kipling, Rudyard (1936), "If," recovered from *The Book of Virtues,* William J. Bennett, Editor (New York: Simon and Schuster, 1993), pp. 476-477.

5. Shenk, p. 66.

6. Ibid., p. 56.

II. ALTRUISM

Three Cases of Self-Sacrifice

1. Myers, David, *The Pursuit of Happiness: Who Is Happy and Why* (New York: William Morrow and Company, 1992), p. 196.

2. "Mother picks death to continue life through her son." *The Washington Post*, March 7, 1995.

3. Ibid.

4. Stephanie Strom, "Doner wants to give till it hurts." *New York Times News Service*, August 17, 2003.

5. Szasz, Thomas, *The Second Sin* (New York: Doubleday, 1973), p. 67.

6. Rand, Ayn, *The Virtue of Selfishness* (New York: Penguin Books, 1961), pp. vii—xii.

Into the Sun

1. Jamison, Kay Redfield, *An Unquiet Mind* (New York: Random House, 1995), pp. 11-13.
2. Nouwen, Henri, *Encounters with Merton* (New York: The Crossroad Publishing Company, 1972), p. 42.

III. AUTHENTICITY

What does it mean to be real?

1. Rokeach, Milton, *The Three Christs of Ypsilanti* (New York: Kopf, 1961).
2. Percy, Walker, *Lost in the Cosmos: The Last Self-Help Book* (New York: Washington Square press, 1983), p. 5.
3. Ibid., p. 12.
4. Hawthorne, Nathaniel, *The Scarlet Letter* (New York: Norton, 1978), p. 107.
5. Copyright (1922) expired in USA. Recovered from http://www.mindspring.com/ -mccarthys/cybrary/velvet.htm on August 25, 2006.
6. Masterson, James, *The Search for the Real Self* (New York: The Free Press, 1988), p. 24.

IV. COMPASSION

Illyssa

1. Green, Tim, *A Man and His Mother: An Adopted Son's Search* (New York: Harper Collins), p. 88-90.

A Child Shall Lead Them

1. Bourke, Dale Hansen, *Everyday Miracles: Holy Moments in a Mother's Day* (Dallas, TX: Word Publishing, 1989), pp. 37-43.

V. COURAGE

Heroic Acts

1. *Webster's New World Dictionary* (New York: Simon and Schuster, 1984), p. 325.

2. Ibid., p. 327.

3. Trueblood, Elton, *The Life We Prize* (New York: Harper and Row, 1951), p. 154.

4. Ibid., p. 155.

5. Martin, Mike W., *Everyday Morality: An Introduction to Applied Ethics* (Belmont, CA: Wadsworth Publishing Co., 1989), p. 121.

6. *The Washington Post*, January 13, 1982.

7. Ibid.

8. Wallace, James, "Courage, Cowardice, and Self-Indulgence," *Virtues and Vices* (Ithaca, NY: Cornell University Press, 1978), pp. 78-81.

9. "Courage Under Fire" (2001), 20th Century Fox, Running Time: 125 Minutes.

VII. ENDURANCE

The Ice Bowl

1. *The N.F.L.'s Greatest Games*, "The Ice Bowl," (1997), PolyGram Video, Running Time: 72 Minutes.

2. Myers, David, *Psychology*, Eighth Edition, (New York: Worth Publishers, 2004), p. 221.

3. *The N.F.L.'s Greatest Games*.

4. Ibid.

5. Ibid.

6. Ibid.

7. Ibid.

8. Ibid.

9. Maranass, David, *When Pride Still Mattered* (New York: Simon and Schuster, 1999), p. 416.

10. *The N.F.L.'s Greatest Games*.

11. Ibid.

VIII. FORGIVENESS

The Sunflower

1. Martin, Mike W., *Everyday Morality: An Introduction to Applied Ethics* (Belmont, CA: Wadsworth Publishing Co., 1989), p. 163.
2. Nuland, Sherwin, *How We Die: Reflections on Life's Final Chapter* (New York: Random House, 1993), p. 124.
3. Ibid., p. 128.
4. Luke 14: 25-33.
5. Prager, Dennis, "When Forgiveness Is a Sin," *The Wall Street Journal*, December 15, 1997, p. 38.
6. Luke 23:34.
7. "A Time to Kill, (1996), Warners Brothers, Running Time: 150 Minutes.

IX. HAPPINESS

Who Is Happy and Why?

1. Aristotle, *Ethics* (Translated: J.A.K. Thompson and Hugh Tredennick, New York: Penguin). Recovered from Martin, Mike W., *Everyday Morality: An Introduction to Applied Ethics* (Belmont, CA: Wadsworth Publishing Co., 1989), p. 40.
2. Csikszentmihalyi, Mihalyi, *Flow: The Psychology of Optimal Experience* (New York: Harper Collins, 1990), p. 66.
3. Phelps, Milo Ray, *New Yorker*, December 21, 1929.
4. Prager, Dennis, *Happiness Is a Serious Problem* (New York: Harper and Row, 1998), pp. 31.
5. Recovered from: www.brainyquote/quotes/o/oscarwilde.html on August 18, 2006.
6. Watson, Lillian Eichler, *Light from Many Lamps: A Treasury of Inspiration* (New York: Simon and Schuster, 1951), p.29.
7. Recovered from: pitara at http://www.pitara.com/talespin/poems/online on July 26, 2006.
8. Hauser, Thomas, *Muhammed Ali: His Life and Times* (New York: Simon and Schuster, 1991), p. 310.
9. "The Mystery of Happiness:" *20/20* (January 22, 1998), Avaialble from www.abcnews.com/2020.

X. HUMILITY

Elie Wiesel: An Exceptional Teacher

1. Malikow, Max, "Effective Teacher Study," (Houston, TX: *Teacher Education Journal—Electronic*, Volume 16 Number 3E. National Forum Journals.)

2. Coles, John Robert, "The Disparity Between Intellect and Character," *The Chronicle of Higher Education*, September 22, 1995.

3. Buscaglia, Leonard, *Papa, My Father: A Celebration of Dads* (New York: Wiliam Morrow and Company, Inc., 1989), p. 46.

4. "Dead Poets Society" (1985) Touchstone Home Video. Running Time: 128 Minutes.

XII. INTEGRITY

Francesca's Decision

1. Szasz, Thomas, *The Second Sin* (New York: Doubleday, 1973), p. 47.

2. Waller, Robert James, *The Bridges of Madison County* (New York: Warner Books, 1992), p. 16.

3. *Publishers Weekly.* Recovered from: http://www.amazon.com/gp/product on June 19, 2006 at 12:04 p.m.

4. Waller, pp. 115-116.

5. Ibid.

6. Ibid., pp. 116.

7. Kohlberg, Lawrence, *The Philosophy of Moral Development, Volume I* (San Francisco, CA: Harper and Row, 1981).

8. Szasz, Thomas, *The Second Sin* (New York: Doubleday, 1973), p. 13.

9. "The Bridges of Madison County" (2000) Warner Brothers, Running Time: 135 Minutes.

Joe Louis' Debt

1. McRae, Donald, *Heroes Without a Country* (New York: Harper Collins, 2002), p. 279.

2. Cannon, Jimmy, *The New York Post*, October 26, 1951.

3. McRae, p. 275.

4. Folsom, Burton W., "Joe Louis vs. the IRS" (Mackinac Center for Public Policy) posted July 7, 1997. Recovered from http://www.mackinac.org/article on May 21, 2006.

5. McRae, p. 288.
6. Ibid., p. 297.
7. "The Kings of the Ring," (1995) The Big Fights, Inc. Running Time: 92 Minutes.

XIII. LOYALTY

Uriah

1. Szasz, Thomas, *The Second Sin* (New York: Doubleday, 1973), p. 47.
2. II Samuel 11:1-27.
3. "A Few Good Men," (1992) Columbia Pictures: Columbia Tristar Home Video, Running Time 138 Minutes.

XIV. PERSEVERANCE

Cutting and Running

1. Szasz, Thomas, *The Second Sin* (New York: Doubleday, 1973), p. 49.
2. Aron Ralston, *Between a Rock and a Hard Place* (New York: Simon and Schuster—Atria, 2004).

XV. RESPONSIBILITY

Exploding Pintos

1. "Ford Pinto," Wikepedia. Recovered from http://en.wikipedia.org on July 20, 2006.
2. Ibid.
3. Melden, A.I., *Ethical Theories: A Book of Readings* -Second Edition (Englewood Cliffs, NJ: Prentice Hall), p. 345.
4. "Class Action," (1990) Twentieth Century Fox, Running Time: 110 Minutes.

Addiction and Responsibility

1. Peck, M. Scott, *The Road Less Traveled: A New psychology of Love, Traditional Values and Spiritual Growth* (New York: Simon and Schuster, 1978), pp. 33-34.
2. Szasz, Thomas, *The Second Sin* (New York: Doubleday, 1973), p. 45.

A Teen's Affair

1. Abigail Van Buren, "Teen's affair ends with man in prison." *The Post Standard*, November 4, 2002, p. D-2.

XVI. THOUGHTFULNESS

On Education and E.T.

1. Kreeft, Peter, *The Best Things in Life: A 20th Century Socrates Looks at Power, Pleasure, Truth and the Good Life* (Downers Grove, IL: Inter Varsity Press, 1984), pp. 15-21.
2. Trueblood, Elton, The Life We Prize (New York: Harper and Brothers Publishers, 1951). P. 36.
3. Kreeft.

XVII. WISDOM

Papa, the Educator

1. Buscaglia, Leo, *Papa, My Father: A Celebration of Dads* (New York: William Morrow and Company, Inc., 1989), pp. 42-46.

A Philosopher Almost Commits Suicide

1. Hoffer, Eric, *Truth Imagined* (New York: Harper and Row, Publishers, 1983), p.22.
2. Ibid., p. 24.

3. Ibid., p. 25.

4. "Eric Hoffer Quotes." Recovered from http://www.phnet.fi/public/mamaa1/hoffer.htm on June 27, 2006 at 9:30 a.m.

5. "Eric Hoffer: Biography and Encyclopedia." Recovered from http://www.absoluteastjtsnomy.com on June 27, 2006.

6. Hoffer, p. 93.

7. "Eric Hoffer Quotes."

8. Hoffer. *Truth Imagined*

9. Grollman, Earl A. and Malikow, Max, *Living When a Young Friend Commits Suicide or Is Even Thinking About It* (Boston, MA: Beacon Press, 1999).